HOW TO CONQUER YOURSELF

DISCIPLINE & WILLPOWER FOR THE CONSCIOUS, CREATIVE THINKER

BY BRYAN OGILVIE

COPYRIGHT © 2013 DOTHEKNOWLEDGE.COM

ISBN: 0615821987
ISBN-13: 978-0615821986

"Knowing others is intelligence, but to know yourself is true wisdom.
Conquering others is strength, but to conquer yourself is true power."
~ Lao Tzu

"The two strongest predictors of success are intelligence and self-control."
~ Roy Boymeister, Ph.D.

TABLE OF CONTENTS

INTRODUCTION

I believe that life is meant to be conquered and that a creative, intelligent psyche - a self-aware, self-directed thinker - is an unconquerable force.

To see this force in action, to grasp this creative strength and wield its power in actual life, requires one to both think and act in a disciplined way: to both see the world through a disciplined frame of mind as well as construct one's goals through a disciplined style of behavior. The strength to conquer one's creative potential, therefore, **first begins with the strength to conquer one's self**.

This book will outline such a process: it's a strategic guide to cultivating willpower for the conscious, creative thinker, and aims to help those who see themselves as knowledgeable but yet idle, or inactive; talented but yet lethargic and lax in terms of their actual behavior. This book intends to help creative individuals who suffer from chronic procrastination and lack self-control, hoping to thus terminate the anxiety and confusion such poor habits entail.

For definition purposes, a conscious, creative thinker is an intelligent, independent-minded person who tends to express himself through an artistic activity, or any set of activities which could be deemed so...

A conscious-creative is someone you meet who makes you think, "*Wow, that's a really cool, interesting person.*" Technically, they may be anything from a photographer, songwriter or actress to a stand-up comedian or video-game programmer, but the emphasis here is on their identity - on the unique, creative perspective they take towards (and provide) the world.

Examples include:

- screenwriters

- writers of all sorts

- filmmakers

- photographers

- graphic designers

- social activists

- musicians of all sorts (composers, engineers, percussionists, etc.)

- actors and actresses (voice-actresses or voice-actors)

- painters

- consultants and personal coaches

- spoken-word artists, MC's or street performers

- healthcare practitioners (masseuses, nutritionists, etc.)

…and so on. Although, technically speaking, *anyone* could perform some of the above work - anyone can, for instance, simply *say* they're a painter, poet or filmmaker and then perform the mechanical acts these professions involve - again, the emphasis here is on identity: on the creativity and awareness that emanates from an individual's *personality* alongside their artistic talent and skill.

If this person is you, and if the desire to conquer yourself is a pivotal concern, then this book is yours. "Yours" not simply in the sense of possession of course, but yours in that it exists for you, was written with you in mind and may mark a key transitory shift in your creative career. Enjoy it in good health, and **make use of its contents.**[1]

For any questions - if any passages are unclear, if you have any suggestions or would like to speak with me directly about any of the subject matter contained herein - contact me, bryan@dotheknowledge.com

---

[1] NOTE: To disclaim, nothing that follows is to be construed as medical, legal or psychiatric counsel, nor to be taken as professional advice of any sort whatsoever. For such concerns, seek help from a licensed practitioner whom you trust.

This book began as a compendium of notes for myself; as a way of getting my own act together personally. It's therefore shared as *opinion* and technically classified as *entertainment.*

CH. 1: THE TWO FRONTIERS TO CONQUER

"TO CONQUER YOURSELF IS TO BE AT TACTICAL WAR AGAINST BOTH
YOUR INSTINCTS AND YOUR SOCIAL CONDITIONING, SIMULTANEOUSLY."

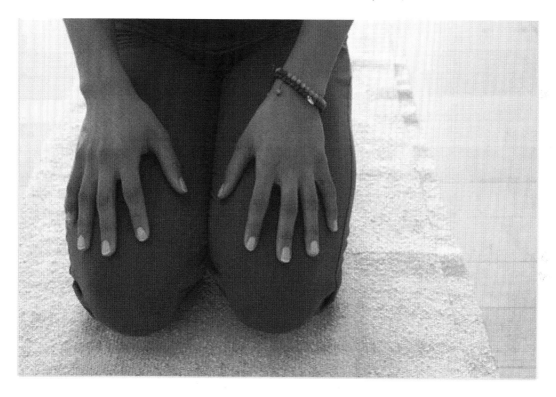

"The chains of habit are too light to be felt until they're too heavy to be broken."
~ Samuel Johnson

*"Society is in constant flux, but the majority conform to whatever is normal for
the time and play the role allotted to them."* ~ Robert Greene

THE 2 KEY ASPECTS TO CONQUER

There are two key aspects to conquering yourself. By "aspects," I mean that there are two key pivotal concerns, two key fundamental ideas, around (and upon) which *the ambition* to conquer yourself revolves (and rests). **The first of these two aspects is "internal"** because it represents challenges that are personal, psychological or otherwise found inside you as an individual, whereas **the second is "external"** because it represents challenges that are social, environmental or otherwise found in our collective world.

In other words, half of conquering yourself is about your own human nature, while the other half to conquering yourself is about our culture; about how culture and civilization then sets *the context* within which that human nature is made to unfold. We'll spend this rest of this chapter detailing the specific dynamics that govern each of these halves.

So what at first seems like a complex process - a procedural guide to overcoming procrastination, attaining discipline, cultivating willpower and so on - really breaks down to these two key prepositions. Let's go further in depth…

WILLPOWER IS AN INDIRECT GAME (INTERNAL CONCERNS)

The first, internal concern, *"Willpower is an indirect game,"* means that the *internal* aspect to conquering yourself (everything that you can influence and control personally, such as your level of willpower, motivation and productivity) is best handled by methods that are indirect and counter-intuitive, never obvious or straightforward.

"Willpower is an indirect game" because willpower, for the most part, is determined by factors that we're typically *unaware of*. We have to use an indirect process to attain willpower because it's governed by dynamics we don't intuitively understand.

Specifically, willpower is <u>not</u> a direct game because *human behavior, as a whole, <u>is not</u> the direct result of conscious will* or of any rational, decision-making process. To the contrary, for the most part, human behavior is an indirect *by-product* of subconscious emotions and instinctual drives which we tend to remain oblivious to.

Again, **almost everything we do as humans is a by-product of instinctual drives and subconscious processes**, not conscious "will" or rational thinking, which is why trying to force or compel discipline out of yourself (or out of anyone else for that matter) - trying to coerce yourself to be more productive, have more ambition or stop procrastinating - simply doesn't work.

Regardless of the stakes involved, and regardless of how important or promising a creative project may be, direct force is almost always the ineffective and counter-productive approach to take. For instance...

- simply demanding yourself to wake up earlier won't remove you from the comfort of your bed at the time you'd like to

- simply forcing yourself to exercise daily won't motivate you to stay with a routine more than a few weeks (if that) and

- simply deciding, even with full resolve and conscious intent, to write and direct a new screenplay won't convert itself into a finished cinematic product.

In fact, these methods can even be thought of as unsophisticated and naive, as they ignore the subtle dynamics that actually determine human behavior to begin with.[1]

Take a look at everything you've done for the past twenty-four hours: everything from the time you got out of bed, the way you brushed your teeth, what you ate for breakfast, what happened at work or at school, what you did on your lunch break, the time you got home, the music you listened to on your iPod and anything else you did to wind down or replenish yourself.

Now *take a look at those same twenty-four hours on an emotional or psychological level:* how did you feel and think throughout it? What was your general mood? If you had several moods, what where

---

[1] Most people mistakenly think of willpower and discipline as character traits; as part of their personality they either have or don't have enough of (no different than honesty or confidence). This mistaken view then takes their attention away from where it should be - away from the real mechanics involved - and places it on their own identity, which can lead to having the negative *self-image* of an undisciplined or weak-willed person, a much more difficult problem to resolve. In this way, *mistaking willpower for a character trait convolutes the entire concern,* and can lead people to feel defeated and helpless rather than motivated or encouraged to change.

they and at what times did you experience them? What were the tone, style and subject matter of your conversations? Which coworkers, friends and loved ones did you speak with, what worries and anxieties came to mind, and what did you do to escape or alleviate them?

Here's the final question: out of all your actions, experiences, feelings, worries, ideas and decisions, *how much of it was willpower, and how much of it was simply habit and routine?* How much of it was a logical, conscientious choice to do what was most sensible, productive or aligned with your personal goals and how much of it was merely emotional patterns, social pressure and instinctual responses simply playing themselves out while superseding your awareness and control?

My point here is that <u>we human beings are essentially organic machines</u>[2]. I'm not saying this to tarnish or revoke the elegance of being human; only to put willpower in its proper frame and perspective. Specifically, *you can't Conquer Yourself until you see that the "self" you're trying to conquer is an animal first; a creature that acts through routine and responds to animalistic stimuli much more than it does information, reasoning or conscious will,* which is why it's so challenging to conquer in the first place...

In fact, neuroscientist Dr. Paul D. MacLean developed the "Triune Brain Theory" to help explain this[3]. According to the Triune Brain model, our brain's evolution can be categorized into three distinct phases, which, in layman's terms, means that **we humans don't just have one brain, we have three**.

These three brains (or phases) each have their own distinct location in the mind, their own distinct evolutionary function and their own distinct series of biological drives, or needs. They therefore, of course, often compete and conflict with one another.

The three brains are, roughly:

    1. the Human, "Logical" brain (located in the neocortex)

    2. the Mammalian, "Emotional" brain (located in the limbic system and amygdala) and

---

[2] As an exercise, monitor behavior like this over an extended trial period for yourself, anyone close enough for you to honestly observe and then for society as a whole. It'll be both disturbing and enlightening at the same time.

[3] See MacLean's *The Triune Brain in Evolution* for more.

3. the Reptilian, "Physical" brain (located in the basal ganglia)

So for instance, whereas our logical brain strives to create and devise order, our emotional brain strives for a sense of belonging while our physical brain strives only for survival and exhibits territorial behavior. That is, whereas your logical brain is what plans your events and understands what you're reading now, your emotional and physical brains are what govern, say, your dietary choices, your confidence level, relationship patterns and so on.

You can think of this as having separate brains for each the mind, heart and body (the neocortex, limbic system and basal ganglia, respectively), but the point is, while your goals and decision-making willpower capacity reside in your logical intelligence, *the anxieties and apprehensions you have about them reside in more primitive aspects of your evolutionary past*.

Remember, the various drives often compete with one another, and each brain evolved subsequently to the brain underneath it, meaning that the logical came in *after* the emotional, and the emotional itself came in *after* the physical. This being so, logic tends to have the weakest leverage and least influence on our overall behavior.

Human reasoning (which includes the ability to will, discipline or "motivate" yourself to do anything) is the new kid on the block, and has trouble exerting itself without the help of unconscious factors anterior to it. Although we like to deceive ourselves and *believe* that we're logical creatures guided by will, the reality is that almost everything we do, think and feel is governed by dynamics we don't intuitively understand and never naturally detect.

For instance, when young men "sow the wild oats" and pursue women, *it's rarely because they find a girl intelligent, genuinely interesting or to be a healthy, positive influence on their lives* - it's because they have physical desires to sedate and because, emotionally, they just want another notch on their belt to bolster their self-esteem.

When advertising companies design their campaigns, *it's rarely based on why a product is technically superior, cost-effective or an otherwise sensible purchase*, but on the manipulation of their target audience's psyche - they use celebrities to lend their merchandise an aura of significance, or fear-based marketing tactics to trigger anxiety (which their merchandise then proposes to relieve).

Even when individuals are driven to major success, in many cases it's their need for validation - the attention and acceptance they never got from their parents, for instance - which they then look to unconsciously deduct from society as a whole.

So again, willpower is an indirect game: **people act and raise their productivity for reasons they're typically unaware of.** This being so, if you'd like to cultivate willpower, stop thinking through the "direct" lens of motivation, discipline or force but instead, through the *indirect*, counterintuitive lens of psychology, subconscious processes and instinctual drives. For example…

Broadcast Your Commitments: if you'd like to film a documentary or start a blog, simply make an official event for the film debut or website launch and publicize that date. A public deadline creates social pressure that'll impel and coerce performance out of you, simply to maintain your image in the public eye.

You may think this unprincipled, but the reality is that *it works*, and it works because we humans tend to protect our social image better than a comic-book superhero protects his secret identity.

The fear of embarrassment is wired deep into our psyche and may even be related to our fear of social exclusion (for survival purposes) in more tribal, nomadic times. Leverage this dynamic against yourself by broadcasting your commitments publicly.

Conceal Your Diet: if you'd like to eat healthier, if you notice certain foods taking a toll on your creativity, mood or concentration, simply keep healthy choices on display out in visible areas and unhealthy choices concealed in hidden, inconvenient ones. Studies show that when we're hungry, we unconsciously reach for the most accessible item, so reorganize your kitchen to trick your unconscious with this in mind.

Put sweets high up in the cabinet (where they can't be seen) and leave the apples, almonds and so on right out on the table. This'll help make healthy eating more likely, habitual and almost effortless.

The key idea here is to create discipline by reverse-engineering it; by asking, "How can I, given what I know about subconscious drives and human nature, make the result I'm looking for *inevitable?*" or "How can I structure *an environment* or *a situation* that would encourage the result I'm looking for to happen on its own accord?"[4]

Remember, **willpower is an indirect game**: we're essentially organic machines in that our biological impulses (physical needs based on the present) and mammalian wiring (emotional responses based

---

[4] The solutions we'll explore later go much deeper than this, but it's a good way to start conquering the internal frontier. The personal, psychological dynamics inhibiting your creativity demand an approach that runs counter to what you'd naturally think.

on conditioning in the past) are what dominate our decision-making process, not conscious thought (logical reasoning based on, and intended for, the future) or "willpower."

The strategy to conquer yourself therefore, is to align these forces: to build willpower indirectly by working through the instinctual, lesser-evolved aspects of human nature, rather than erroneously thinking you can simply force yourself to override them.

Until you become disenchanted with will - until you realize that most *of your behavior stems from emotional conditioning and biological impulses (not logical thinking), and through a process that happens automatically (not through deliberate choice) - self-discipline will always elude you. You may even come to interpret your lack of willpower as a personal fault or some defect of character, rather than merely as a lack of knowledge.*

Once more, willpower is an indirect game. Work to build it indirectly through the underlying, counterintuitive factors that truly determine it, not through the old-fashioned delusion of force.

THE SUBTLE CONSPIRACY AGAINST SELF-DISCIPLINE

Lastly, the second, external frontier, "*There's a subtle conspiracy against self-discipline,*" means that the challenge to conquer yourself is further complicated by living in a culture antagonistic to it. "There's a subtle conspiracy against self-discipline" because society itself is structured in ways that impede and sabotage your attempts to attain it; and we can think of this as "a conspiracy" because the ways in which it does so are both widespread and systematic, yet subtle and obscure.

Ironically, whereas the American tradition once centered around an ethic of thrift and industriousness, it's now mutated into a culture of sloth and indulgence. So becoming privy to this trend - devising means to prevent it from developing within yourself - is as critical to building discipline in the digital age as any of the more personal, internal dynamics involved.

Again, beyond learning to leverage your unconscious in ways that favor willpower, there also lies an additional challenge: shielding such leverage from the social conditioning and societal norms most likely to inhibit it, which include (A) the cultural bias towards entertainment, (B) the cultural bias towards distraction and (C) the cultural bias towards surface level thinking. Let's discuss:

Our cultural bias towards entertainment, or "the culture of entertainment" for short, refers to the subtle way in which *media-programming has turned us into a society more concerned with entertaining ourselves than we are with getting results.* For instance, our fascination with…

- celebrity gossip

- reality TV

- professional wrestling

- internet memes and

- the gaming apps on our mobile devices

...are all examples of how <u>we're conditioned to orient our lives around diversion and leisure rather than discipline and personal accomplishment</u>.

So we have to train ourselves to not get lost or too absorbed in these amusements, because, "We've transformed our culture into a vast replica of Pinocchio's Pleasure Island, where boys were lured with the promise of no school and endless fun. They were all, however, turned into donkeys - a symbol in Italian culture of ignorance and stupidity."[5]

Our cultural bias towards distraction, or simply our culture *of* distraction, refers to the subtle way in which *technology has turned us into a society in which the inability to focus has become the norm*. For instance, our dependence on, and literal obsession with...

- smartphone gadgetry

- text messaging

- email alerts

- social network notifications and

- Skype or "Face-Time" video-calls that disturb us at any given moment

---

[5] Chris Hedges in his 2010 work, *Empire of Illusion*.

...are all examples of how <u>we're conditioned for attention-deficit disorder and *disorderliness* rather than clarity and concentration</u>.

So we have to train ourselves to eliminate and minimize distraction and interruption, because, "As our culture becomes more mobile, high-speed, techno-stressed, information-cluttered and media-saturated, we're getting pushed out of our ability to focus without even noticing it."[6]

Our cultural bias towards surface-level thinking, or our culture *of* superficiality, refers to the subtle way in which *consumerism has turned us into a society that values experiences only in shallow and artificial form*. For instance...

- constantly snacking instead of eating full meals

- downloading individual songs instead of full albums (and switching incessantly through literally *thousands* of songs on our MP3 players)

- buying books but reading only the first chapter and

- having hundreds of online "friends" but few, if any, meaningful connections in the real world

...are all examples of how <u>we're conditioned to rush impatiently through things rather than finish and process them completely</u>.

So we have to train ourselves to go deeper in order to obtain results and get the full "nutrition" an experience contains because, "If you obsessively snack on things - whether they be food, goals, relationships or even learning, such as in a program like this - you're missing out on eighty to ninety percent of the value."[7]

Here, of course, I only mean "conspiracy" in the allegorical sense. None of this is to criticize the world, suggest that it intentionally conspires against you or promote a victim mentality, but only to highlight the specific trends most detrimental to your productivity that (similar to the aspects of

---

[6] Lucy Jo Palladino in her book, *Find Your Focus Zone*.

[7] Eben Pagan in his video-training program, *Wake Up Productive*.

human nature that supersede will) tend to operate beyond our awareness. It's simply a framework to help you conquer yourself.

Aside from these three primary biases however, there are many more, such as **the cultural bias towards fear**, or an unconscious social *climate* of fear in our modern society as well…

- news media, with its focus on crime, terrorism and natural disasters

- the cosmetic and pharmaceutical industries, with their focus on disease and physical appearance and even

- religious movements, with their focus on hell, eternal damnation and apocalyptic disaster

…all center around, and rely on, the promotion of fear, because a person who's fearful and terrified is also far easier to persuade, influence and control.[8] This subtle environment of fear, terror and anxiety should be on every conscious and creative individual's radar as another factor to be vigilant against; to mentally "vaccinate" himself from.

Again, *there's a subtle conspiracy against self-discipline.* Your ability to detect this, to devise means of shielding and counterattacking it's effect on you, is as critical for building discipline in the digital age as any of the more personal, internal dynamics involved.

REFERENCES AND FURTHER CONCERNS...

For more on the cultural biases of entertainment, distraction and superficial thinking, see *Empire of Illusion: The End of Literacy and the Triumph of Spectacle* by Chris Hedges, *Find Your Focus Zone: An Effective New Plan to Defeat Distraction and Overload* by Lucy Jo Palladino, and *The Hidden Persuaders* by Vance Packard, respectively.[9]

---

[8] As a critical thinking exercise, what other "cultural biases" and "conspiracies against self-discipline" can you imagine, given your own experience and outlook towards the world? How do these, along with some of the biases previously mentioned, affect, limit or hinder your sense of self-control?

[9] Of all these, I find Hedges's work the most eloquent and far reaching.

For more on the triune model of neurological function (the three minds), see *The Triune Brain in Evolution: Role of the Paleocerebral Functions* by Dr. Paul D. MacLean, or, as a more layman overview of the same, *The Dragons of Eden: Speculations on the Evolution of Human Intelligence* by Paul Sagan.

Keep these two frontiers in mind as you continue to read and always relate the advice, solutions and strategies back to them. You'll find this reinforces the learning at a deeper level and will lead you to develop insights and practical techniques on your own accord.

Once more, there are two frontiers to conquer - two interacting battlegrounds which all problems with creative self-discipline emanate from...

1.) <u>Internal challenges</u> that are personal or psychological in nature, conquered by understanding that *willpower is an indirect game* and

2.) <u>External challenges</u> that are social or environmental in scope, conquered understanding that *there's a subtle conspiracy against self-discipline*.

As a result, **to conquer yourself is to be at tactical war with both your instincts *and* your social conditioning, simultaneously**. Just remember that you'll need strategies to address both concerns.

Take a break to reflect and let's continue...

CH. 2: HOW TO END PROCRASTINATION

"PROCRASTINATION BEGINS BY CONFUSING YOUR ACCOMPLISHMENTS
WITH WHAT YOUR PERSONAL VALUE IS AS A HUMAN BEING…"

"Stop making identity meaning out of external events…" ~ Eben Pagan

*"Free yourself from an attitude about your worth and abilities that are
inappropriate for your current age, intellect and power."*
~ Neil Fiore, PhD

THE PROCRASTINATOR'S DILEMMA (VISUALIZATION)

We'll start this chapter with a visualization exercise, "The Procrastinator's Dilemma," to introduce my framework of how procrastination operates. Afterwards, we'll dissect the visualization as a metaphor - as an allegory *symbolizing* the habit of procrastination as a whole - in order to devise strategies that'll break this habit at its root. As simple as it may seem, follow this process thoroughly to end the procrastination now blocking your creative productivity once and for all.

[SCENARIO A] Imagine I placed a plank on the ground - a wooden board about ten feet long, two feet wide and only a few inches thick - and asked you to walk across it as it laid there.

How would you respond? You'd probably do it without hesitation of course. You might laugh at the whole idea and find it pointless, but as long as there was nothing to suspect you'd perform it effortlessly.

[SCENARIO B] Now imagine I took this same wooden plank but *suspended it between two Manhattan high-rises, more than 200 ft. over concrete pavement* and <u>then</u> asked you to walk across it.

How would you respond here? What are you saying to yourself this time?

"No thanks..." right?

"I might fall," or,

"The wind might knock me over..."

This time, your feelings about the task have changed because <u>the potential consequences</u> (i.e. falling to your most-certain death) have changed, and this shift in potential consequences has caused you to lose sight of how simple the task actually is.

In this second instance, it's no longer a playful test or just a game, <u>it's risking your life</u>. Adrenaline rushes through you as you visualize yourself falling twenty-plus stories down, you're no longer calm and there's nothing to laugh at anymore.

Notice how the thought, "*If I make a mistake I could die,*" makes it impossible for you to take action.

[SCENARIO C] And lastly, in this same situation (a plank suspended sky-high between towers), imagine that as you stand there paralyzed by the thought of crossing, the building you're currently standing on *catches fire*.

How would you respond here? <u>You're entire focused changed</u>, didn't it? Now you're going to *find* a way to get across no matter what, and the thought of not doing it perfectly never even comes to mind. You may of gotten creative and said:

"I'd just sit down on the board and scoot my behind over to the other end," or

"I'd crawl on my hands and knees if I had to."

But what happened here??? Why did your feelings change so quickly? How did you go from worry, ambivalence and procrastination to productivity and creative problem-solving in mere seconds???

In simple terms, the "possibility" of pain and death became <u>the certainty</u> of pain and death…*that's* what impelled you to take action and <u>that's also precisely what happens when we procrastinate</u>.[1]

THE PROCRASTINATOR'S DILEMMA (EXPLAINED)

In our minds, **we act out scenario B (raise the plank) when we falsely associate our success with our sense of personal value,** and in our actual lives, **we <u>create</u> scenario C (notice the fire) as a result of that initial procrastination.**

That is, *underlying our procrastination is a mistaken, subliminal connotation between what we do and <u>what our intrinsic value is</u> as a human being.*

---

[1] The formal, complete version of this exercise can be found in Dr. Neil Fiore's book *The Now Habit.*

On a deeper level, you "suspend planks between skyscrapers" by unconsciously translating a task into a measurement of who you are: into evidence as to whether or not you're acceptable and into forecasts of what will become of you into the future.

Once you confuse your performance with your identity like that, "finishing this screenplay," "starting this business," "passing this exam," "getting this job," and even "dating this person" get inflated with a level of significance that makes failure (and even slight mistakes) seem like the end of the world; unbearable and cataclysmic, like psychological equivalents to falling off of a Manhattan high-rise.

This leads to perfectionism, where error, criticism and rejection become emotionally comparable to death: you'll demand yourself to do things perfectly in order for your audience to accept you completely, and this expectation is what freezes you in the confines of self-judgment, inertia and anxiety.

Remember, anxiety, strictly as a biological response, occurs when an organism perceives eminent danger or any threat to its survival. Here, ironically, it occurs when a person *imagines* failure and its fictitious, exaggerated ramifications - a "threat to survival" in the metaphorical sense - such as:

- losing your position or social standing

- being publicly criticized or condemned

- never finding employment again

- separating your family

…and so on. This anxiety is then evaded through procrastination which, as a coping mechanism, accomplishes a variety of things:

1. it allows us to escape the dilemma and feel a sense of temporary relief

2. it brings the deadline closer (the urgent, scenario C "fire"), which, by scaring us into action, thereby frees us from the responsibility to make a decision [2] and lastly

---

[2] Since procrastination motivates us, makes decisions for us, gets us to act and overrides our perfectionism, it also unconsciously reinforces the belief that procrastination makes sense and has its rewards (hence the saying, "I work best under pressure." and so on).

3. by delaying a task long enough, it no longer becomes a measurement of our true capabilities; what we "could of done" if we "had enough time."

...in this way, **procrastination naturally suits our already inborn tendency towards self-deception**.[3] So instead of all this, try:

[SCENARIO D] Imagine you're on the plank once more, but there's no fire this time, and you're not on top of any high-rises. Instead, *you're in between two small, single-floor cottages, and there's a huge net*: a strong, supportive safety net right under the board.

How would you respond here?

"It's nothing," isn't it?

If anything happened, you'd just fall right into the net, and it might even be fun.

In similar fashion, let go of your perfectionist urge: know that making a mistake does *not* mean death, and in fact means nothing at all. Maximize your performance and overcome procrastination by creating a sense of self-worth independent of your accomplishments, because until you do so, energy and concentration will siphon off from your creative work and go into preparing for imaginary threats to your existence.

PROCRASTINATION AS A COPING MECHANISM

Again, to reinforce, **procrastination is a coping mechanism in response to anxiety** - it's a way to cope *with* anxiety through escape, or, more accurately, a way to gain temporary *relief* from the anxiety a particular task, goal or decision engenders (particularly tasks that require creativity, originality and exposure).

So when we procrastinate, we're not just evading work: underneath that, we're evading the series of fears, threats and risks we unconsciously associate with it. Procrastination is simply the means of carrying out and disguising such an evasion.

---

[3] Tony Schwartz, founder and CEO of The Energy Project, says, "Human beings have an *infinite* capacity for self-deception," an idea we'll explore later in this book.

- If you're cleaning and organizing your desk (though it's already clean and organized) or watching YouTube documentaries (about subjects you're already familiar with) rather than outlining the first draft for your book idea, you're distracting yourself and procrastinating.

- If you're calling up friends or compulsively checking email rather than following up on an important networking opportunity, you're distracting yourself and procrastinating.

- And if you're wandering around with your buddies or spending countless hours in front of the television rather than searching for employment, you're distracting yourself and procrastinating.

But in all of these cases, you're not distracting yourself and procrastinating because you don't *want* a finished book, a wider network of professional contacts or a job (if you didn't, you wouldn't have set such goals to begin with, and the procrastination wouldn't frustrate you either). To the contrary, you're distracting yourself and procrastinating because you don't want *to face* the anxieties, apprehensions and fears these tasks induce, or represent.

Once more, *procrastination is a coping mechanism in response to anxiety*: when we procrastinate, we're not just evading work, we're evading a series of fears we unconsciously associate with it, such as...

- *the fear of failure*, or, more specifically, the fear of embarrassment, shame and catastrophe we assume failure will bring about

- *the fear of success*, or the fear that even if we do succeed, the success will itself bring yet greater challenges and demands which'll expose our limitations and inevitable lead to failure anyway

- *the fear of criticism*, or the fear that we'll be ridiculed and condemned for standing out and simply sharing our views

- *the fear of rejection*, or the fear that we'll no longer be accepted - that we'll be excluded from the social sphere because of our behavior

...and many more, but what's interesting is that **the weight and power these fears have over us -** the extent to which we're made immobile and procrastinate because of them - **stems from the way in which we read both failure and success as indicators of personal value**.

While fear and anxiety are natural, it doesn't follow that they *must* influence your behavior or inhibit your ambition. But if they *are* - if any of this chapter makes sense to you - then it's likely that you've misconstrued your performance to be an accurate source of self-evaluation. For example:

- A new real-estate agent may fear prospecting because he doesn't want to be rejected, but that fear will only stop him if he misconstrues it personally: if he interprets rejection as a sign of his own personal flaws or human inadequacy.

- A young man may fear approaching women because he doesn't want to be embarrassed (rejected in a public setting), but that fear will only stop him if he internalizes it: if he misconstrues embarrassment as a sign of personal shortcoming or sexual undesirability on his part

...and so on. In this way, while fears cause us to procrastinate, *it's how we misinterpret our performance (as a barometer of personal value) that lies behind the strength and authority of those fears.*

You end procrastination, therefore, by ending this senseless and defective link: by creating an unquestionable sense of worth for yourself and by separating that intrinsic, preordained value from whatever successes or failures you happen to experience.

Remember, people don't procrastinate simply because they're lazy, careless or irrational, <u>but because it helps them cope with anxiety and evade (what they perceive as) eminent and terminal danger</u>. In this sense, procrastination then becomes useful to their subconscious and to their self-image, given how vulnerable they are to criticism, failure, rejection and so on.

REFERENCES AND FURTHER CONCERNS...

Lastly, just as there are two frontiers to conquer, there are two types of procrastination as well, or two different *reasons* we procrastinate *for.* The first reason is the one we've just discussed (as a coping mechanism in response to anxiety); the second is what we'll analyze now.

The second reason we procrastinate stems from what psychologists call "resistance to authority," or the deep, emotional need we all have to exert our independence, maintain a sense of freedom, and feel "in control" of our own lives.

Essentially, most adult procrastination isn't that much different than childhood procrastination, because most of an adult's life and a child's life center around the same principle: being *commanded* and *told* what to do.

A young child - an able-bodied, energetic and self-aware being, with it's own conscious will and intent, mind you - is told:

- to go to school

- to do his homework

- to do his chores

- when to come inside

- what to spend his free time doing

- who to spend his free time with

....and so on, and since he can't refuse or disagree, he has no recourse *except* procrastination whenever he's in dissent, so he'll:

- play video games for hours before even starting his homework

- take excessive television breaks as he's doing it

- rush through his chores (barely washing the dishes and leaving them dirty, for instance)

- rarely ever clean his room,

- stay out past curfew

...and so on, but *underlying this unproductive behavior is a need for autonomy* - the need to feel that he has some sense of control or say in his own existence[4].

Both at school and at home, a child's life usually revolves around being commanded, instructed, ordered and compelled. So in time, everything he "has to do" comes to feel like a forced directive and, as discussed in the introduction, force, compulsion and coercion simply don't work over the long term.

Whenever someone's *forced* to do something against their will, they tend to do it poorly, slowly, carelessly, haphazardly or not at all, <u>as inefficiency then becomes their only means of expressing dissent</u>. Here, procrastination, rather than a coping mechanism for anxiety, is thus a passive-aggressive response: a way of getting back at those who order you around because you have no other alternative.

My point here is that this pattern of behavior can transfer into adulthood as well: if, as a child, you never experienced a sense of personal freedom, as an adult, you'll never approach tasks with a sense of ownership, enterprise or personal initiative either. (You'll also have trouble negotiating, stating your preferences and more).

Don't blame your parents for any of the internal issues you have now; simply take note of how these dynamics work and use it to help you make changes as needed.

So again, *there are really two key functions, or purposes, for procrastination*, either:

- as a coping mechanism in response to anxiety, or

- as a passive-aggressive behavior pattern in response to being compelled.

---

[4] None of this is meant to suggest or condemn any particular parenting style, only to clarify that much of our procrastination, as adults, has its roots early in childhood life.

...the first is a method for *escaping distress*; the second is a way of saying, *"You can't make me."*[5]

Furthermore, the first function usually applies to career goals which call for ambition, like finishing a novel, getting into graduate school or starting a photography business; the second to mundane tasks we're simply obligated to perform, like getting to work on time, memorizing complex formulas for a college exam or paying bills.

Since this book is about gaining discipline for creative pursuits, we'll focus more so on the first of course, but it's good to have both causes in mind, so as to not misinterpret *all* habits of procrastination through a singular lens.

For more on procrastination (in both senses, and amongst other diagnoses), see Dr. Neil Fiore's *The Now Habit: A Strategic Program for Ending Procrastination and Enjoying Guilt-Free Play.*

Fiore asserts that **"The self-talk of procrastinators is often about feelings of victimhood, burden and resistance to authority.** By learning to challenge and replace your negative internal dialogue, you'll free yourself from an attitude about your worth and abilities *inappropriate* for your current age, intellect and power."

So as a forerunner to that read, always replace the internal dialogue of "I have to," or "I should" with *"I want to," "I decide,"* or *"I choose."*

The phrase *"I have to"* tends to enkindle feelings of stress and resistance; the implication is that you don't really want to do it, but you still *"have to"* against your will because of external compulsion and as a matter of force.

"I have to" creates an unconscious conflict between maintaining your freedom and handling a specific task (like setting up a payment plan, going to court, renewing your driver's license, etc.); a conflict which can then easily lead you to ambivalence and procrastination.

Likewise, the phrase *"I should"* tends to enkindle feelings of blame, burden and failure. When you say "I should," you're essentially comparing your ideal state to your actual one, and so the phrase is

---

[5] We human beings are interesting creatures in that, whenever we have freedom, we tend to cower in fear and indecision, but whenever we *don't* have freedom, we rebel and resist with indignation and pride. If you pay close attention, you'll notice this subtle form of hypocrisy governing almost all human affairs.

similar to envy (which compares an admired person to the actual you) and longing for the future (which compares an imagined, blissful scenario to the actual present).

Taken too far, saying *"I should"* sends the subliminal idea, *"I'm bad. Where I am is bad. My level of progress is bad, and nothing is the way it should be;"* an idea which can then easily lead you to despair.

Most importantly, *"I have to"* and *"I should"* <u>do not</u> send a clear picture to the mind of:

- *what* you choose to do

- *when* you choose to do it and

- *how* choose to start

...in contrast, *"I choose"* is a language that focuses on results rather than blame, on what *is* rather than what should be and on self-direction rather than external force.

"I choose" subconsciously aligns rather than conflicts, **as it expels the mental judge of internalized parenting.** What you "should" or "have" to do is then replaced by the freedom and responsibility to <u>choose</u> amongst several alternatives.

Again, always replace phrases like, *"I have to"* and *"I should"* with the language of *"I want to," "I decide,"* or *"I choose,"* and remember that your value as a person can never be measured by your achievements - that while your desire for success is healthy, the false notion that your degree of success can ever measure your personal significance *is not.*

Take a break to reflect and let's continue…

CH. 3: HOW TO ATTAIN DISCIPLINE

"WE'RE MOST DISCIPLINED WHEN WE AIM TO MASTER A SKILL,
NOT WHEN WE AIM TO SIMPLY COLLECT A REWARD."

"Before you can do things for people, you must be the kind of man who can get things done. But to get things done, you must love the doing, not the people - your own work, not any possible object of your charity." ~ Ayn Rand

DISCIPLINE BEGINS AS A DESIRE FOR MASTERY

Discipline has several key definitions, two of which, once merged together, become most apt for our purposes here. Let's take a look…

The first key way to define discipline is *"controlled behavior,"* or what we'll refer to as *discipline in the general sense.* This usage can be found in sentences such as, "I should *discipline* myself to eat better," or "His parents spanked him as a child to instill *discipline.*"

The second key way to define discipline is *"an activity that provides mental or physical training,"* or what we'll refer to as *discipline in the specific sense.* This usage can be found in sentences such as, "He mastered several of the martial arts *disciplines,*" or "Yoga has become both a popular exercise routine and a respected spiritual *discipline* here in America."

So sometimes when we use the word discipline, we're referencing *the principle* of self-control (in general), but at other times, we use the word discipline to reference a *specific* activity (in particular), and the logic I want you to grasp here is that **discipline, in the general sense, generally requires** *a* **discipline, in the specific sense, to sustain and exhibit itself through.**

That is, you can't be focused and dedicated over the long-term without a specific craft or creative skill to be focused <u>on</u> and dedicated <u>for</u>. Whether it's drumming in a marching band, practicing karate in a dojo or mastering Italian cuisine in the kitchen, you'll always need a particular path - a singular channel of mastery - to hone in on and centralize your efforts around.

This is why people can show extraordinary amounts of discipline for individual goals and specific events while still lacking even the most basic sense of discipline in their regular lives…

It's why famous, record-breaking magicians like David Blane can discipline themselves for death-defying stunts (like *Frozen in Time,* where he remained submerged in a block of ice for two-and-a-half *days,* or *Vertigo,* where he stood on a 100-ft high pillar in Bryant Park for over *thirty-five hours*), still admit to having trouble managing their diet whenever showtime isn't right around the corner.

It's why critically-acclaimed, world-class performers like Amanda Palmer, who, before her commercial success, *used to pose daily as a living statue,* can discipline themselves to stand perfectly motionless for literally hours on end, yet still suffer from oversleeping and other poor tendencies no different than you or I.[1]

And it's why:

- professional athletes

- star actors

- well-known politicians

- corporate executives

…and other public figures end up as front-page news for undercover scandals that tarnish and soil what would otherwise be a highly-disciplined, extremely focused and well-dignified career. It's why health clubs and gyms are packed with trainees *right before summer begins* and why college libraries are packed with their entire student body *only during the last week of finals.*

(It's also why this chapter may be more significant than any other: the discipline you establish here, the distinct skill-set you choose to master and conquer yourself through, will become the platform and central set of concerns all the other subject matter applies to and operates upon.)

Again, **discipline, in the general sense, generally requires *a* discipline, in the specific sense, in order to sustain and exhibit itself through**, a discipline you have a certain obsession, talent, honor or infatuation for. Here's a more personal analogy…

In my life, my most rewarding relationships weren't the ones where I dated the prettiest girl in school to gain popularity and validation, or the relationships I pursued simply for sex to fill gaps in my self-esteem. My most rewarding relationships were the ones where I genuinely appreciated the girl for who she was as a person: the ones I wanted for nature of the woman herself, pursued from a state of respect and then built a connection, over time, based upon that.

---

[1] These examples are from the first few chapters in Roy Baumeister's *Willpower: Rediscovering the Greatest Human Strength,* a book whose concepts we'll explore thoroughly in Chapter 7.

Discipline works in a similar way: your most rewarding goals - the ones you'll actually be disciplined enough to accomplish - won't be the ones where you'll achieve social status or validation through fame, or the goals you pursue simply for money because you're in a desperate spot. <u>Your most rewarding goals will be the ones you genuinely appreciate for the nature of what they entail</u>; the ones you look at as an honorable craft to develop skill and finesse within, and then build proficiency, over time, based upon that.

So in this respect, *real* discipline begins as a desire for mastery. Technically speaking, discipline could then perhaps be defined *as* mastery itself, making the words…

- discipline

- mastery

- practice

- training

- expertise and

- craftsmanship

…essentially synonymous with one another.

To attain discipline, therefore, is to actually reverse engineer long-term motivation without realizing it. as persistence, determination, dedication and commitment are all natural offsets to this type of fixation. You'll stay loyal to a goal that revolves around mastery because you'll be addicted to the process and behaviors it necessitates and involves.

That's why you're most disciplined when you aim to master a skill, not simply collect a reward. Conversely, if you have a reward in mind (like a financial goal or weight-loss target), without dedication to the particular skill underlying its attainment (like professional accounting or Bodyweight Calisthenics), **you're someone who wants to go somewhere without traveling the path that destination requires**, and you're also nominating yourself for frustration because *the results an effort obtains are rarely, if ever, directly proportional to the <u>amount</u> of effort one invests in order to obtain them.*

RESULTS AREN'T DIRECTLY PROPORTIONAL TO EFFORT

Again, the results we obtain in life are rarely, if ever, directly proportional to the amount of time, energy or money we invest in order to obtain them, *although we tend to assume this as the case*. That is, the creative goals you need discipline for aren't like the jobs you've been paid for, because the simple fact that you're working *does not* entitle you to compensation, nor will it ever. Let me explain...

In the deep recesses of our minds, we each tend to carry around what's known as "a sense of entitlement" and as this sense of of entitlement unconsciously transfers onto our personal aims - our career goals, creative efforts, romantic relationships and so on - it undermines and sabotages the discipline such aims require.

If you were to loosely graph this dynamic, the job-oriented, employee-styled mentality we each tend to take towards our creative efforts and their (presupposed) rate of return, it would look something like this:

The Sense of Entitlement (Employee Thinking)

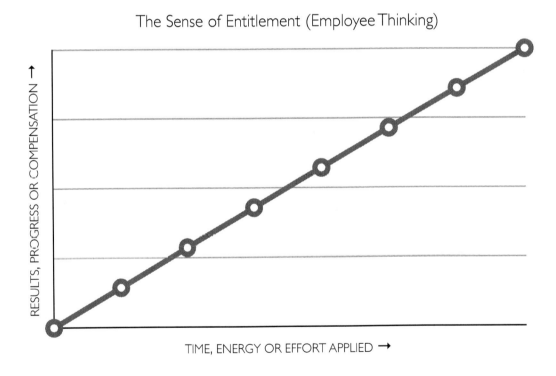

As the graph shows, we *assume* (key word) that we'll progress and gain in at least somewhat direct relation to the amount of time or energy we invest, similar to how an employee is paid directly, and merely, for showing up and working, **but this is a false assumption**. The *reality*, which you can confirm through your own experience, usually graphs out more like this:

The Reality of Results (Disciplined Thinking)

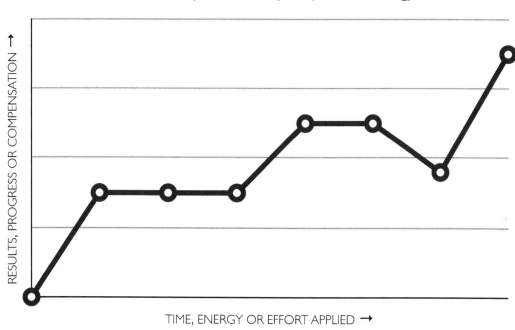

That is, not only do we *not* make as much progress as we'd expect to - as much money, as much exposure or even as much artistic progress in terms of pure skill - but **our journeys consist mostly of plateaus, and even occasional drops, amidst that growth and progression.**

It's not that effort and results don't correlate at all, just that <u>the direct relationship we presume they'll have from the outset is a delusion</u>; a delusion which places us in an emotional cycle of futility and hopelessness, rather than the more logical, mature cycle of continuous, disciplined behavior that results, in reality, require.

Think of the video games you used to play as a child: did you breeze through each one of them effortlessly, or pass maybe only the first two or three stages before being stuck for weeks on the fourth? Could your progress in the game be measured in direct proportion to the amount of time you played it or not, and did you notice that *the difficulty rises, sometimes exponentially, as you progress?*

Think back to the sports, martial arts or musical instruments you trained and rehearsed for: did the various forms, routines, scales or passages come to you naturally, or gradually grow more complex (esoteric even) over time? Did your progress with musical talent or athletic activity or martial art match *exactly* with the amount of energy you spent practicing, or were you not continuously "trapped" at a certain level of ability before reaching the next?

When it comes to getting results, or developing mastery in any form actually, *the difficulty tends to rise, sometimes exponentially, as you advance.* Because of this nearly immutable fact, the best attitude to have, the constructive style (and approach) that maintains focus and discipline in spite of the setbacks inherent to the process, is the desire for mastery. The desire to master a game, martial art, instrument or physical ability for its own sake - for love of the skills and principles they're based on, *not* just the desire to entertain yourself, get a black belt or say, "I'm in a band" - are what create persistence.

Since results aren't directly proportional to effort, think realistically about your progress and creative work with a style of focus that complements such realistic thinking, and always value the cultivation of skill over and above any reward, title or peripheral payoff.

In essence, we lack discipline because we're impatient…it's a cultural phenomenon we'll explore shortly; **the relationship we *assume* effort and results should have with one another - a steady, predictable upward climb - is purely delusional.** Therefore, unless you value a skill on its own, unless you pursue goals with a sense of craftsmanship and patience rather than longing and greed, you'll always lack the commitment and dedication true progress entails.

Remember, *progress is like a woman who respects herself: if all you want her for is her body, you'll never obtain it*, but if you want to develop the best relationship with her you possibly can - if she sees that genuine love driving you - her heart, mind and body become yours for the taking.

Here's that chart once more, with both the delusion and the reality overlapping:

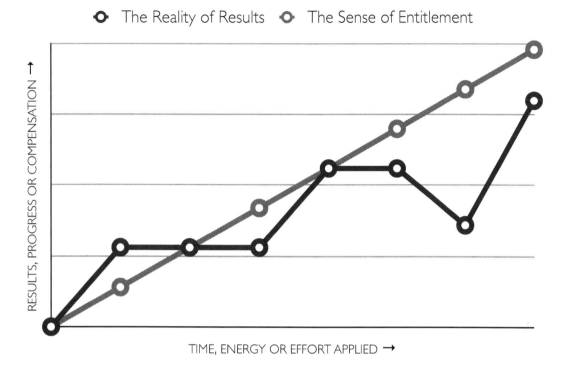

One last time, the results we obtain are rarely, if ever, directly proportional to the time, energy or effort we invest in order to obtain them, though we tend to assume this as the case. *In reality, not only do we not make as much progress as we'd initially expect to, but our experience tends to consist mostly of plateaus (and even occasional drops) amidst that growth and progression.*

This being so, discipline as the desire for mastery becomes the only sensible, realistic and advantageous perspective to have. It's another reason why discipline, in the general sense, generally requires *a* discipline, in the specific sense, in order to sustain and exhibit itself through, so for example:

- if you're a student, seek to master subjects that will soon become key components of your professional career, not just get a high GPA or secure accolades

- if you're a writer, seek to master English prose and become a great novelist, biographer or news correspondent, not just sell books and

- if you're a musician, seek to master your instrument, stage presence and other related aspects of true musicality, not just produce a famous album that'll achieve fame

...etc. etc.

The point is **don't be shallow towards your craft**. Bring a sense of honor towards it instead and you'll morph into a disciplined person without the sense of drudgery a high-level of focus is typically misconstrued to entail.

This isn't to say you shouldn't have material goals, nor to suggest material gain as innately immoral; only that if you want to attain discipline, you'll need to cherish skill and proficiency over success and those more external, tangible rewards.[2]

However, this type of approach is difficult to sustain because it requires what's called

- *"process-oriented" thinking* in a "rewards-oriented" society

- *"delayed-gratification"* in a culture of the more instant variety

- *a focus on life's plateaus* rather than only its peaks and valleys and

- *an overall Eastern perspective* in the midst of an overbearingly Western one.

So here, in essence, to conquer yourself means <u>to become disciplined in an anti-discipline world</u>; to sustain a desire for mastery in a cultural environment *antagonistic* to it. Let's go further in depth…

BECOMING DISCIPLINED IN AN "ANTI-DISCIPLINE" WORLD

Again, if you're in the modern, western world - as in America and everywhere following the American style of existence - you'll need to develop an approach that stems from having an overall *Eastern* perspective while, paradoxically, living in midst a society governed by the consciousness of an overbearingly *Western* one.

In other words, as discussed above, the *amount* of discipline you're able to attain stems from the manner of thinking you take towards progress, and *the two extremes* of this approach stem from either (1) time-honored, traditional values which have their roots in the East, also known as "the

---

[2] In this light, if you're having trouble maintaining discipline, the question to ask yourself then becomes, *"Do I even want to be doing this?"* as you can only be but so focused about an activity you care nothing for.

Orient," or, conversely, (2) more modern, materialistic values which have their roots in Western civilization.

This Western approach, the one you find predominant in American and Eurocentric societies, is *rewards*-oriented; in the Western world you're more likely to find people starting businesses and careers primarily for money, prestige and material gain.

The Eastern approach however, the one you find predominant in East-Asian societies and Indigenous cultures, is *process*-oriented; in the Eastern world you're more likely to find people practicing crafts and communal customs primarily meant for long-term health, spiritual grounding or, as explained, mastery of a skill for its own sake (such as a martial art).

What's interesting, of course, is that the Eastern perspective is *far* more conducive to self-discipline, particularly over the long term, than the Western one, which, of course, is mostly conducive to stress, frustration, burnout and a *lack* of long-term focus and wellbeing. The Eastern perspective understands that life, for the most part, is a series of plateaus, not simply peaks and valleys, and approaches progress with that understanding, whereas the Western perspective conditions us to expect only either major success or tragic failure, and thereby adds a sense of either eagerness or depression to a process such emotions are completely unrelated to.

As a metaphor, you could say that the Eastern approach is that of a calm, Japanese Samurai[3], whereas the Western approach is that of an overexcited, late-night infomercial marketer, promising happiness and sensational dreams through the use of shoddy, typically useless merchandise that couldn't even earn a spot on the sales floor of any decent, respectable retail chain.

So no different than a Japanese Samurai[4], **always bring a sense of code, honor, and principle to your craft in order to cultivate the discipline it necessitates**, regardless of how rare that perspective may be amongst your current friends and associates. At the very least, simply remember that:

> (1) If you're focused only on the rewards you want, you'll lack the patience to truly stick things out, and

---

[3] Hence the use of a Samurai icon as part of this book's cover graphic.

[4] This is what's known as "Bushido Code," which is based on the seven virtues of *Gi* (right action, or duty) *Yuuki* (courage), *Jin* (benevolence), *Rei* (morality, or respect) *Makoto* (truthfulness), *Meiyo* (honor) and *Chuugi* (loyalty). For more, see *The Sword of No-Sword: Life of the Master Warrior Tesshu* by John Stephens or *Bushido: The Soul of Japan* by Inazo Nitobe.

(2) That there are a lot of people who achieve material success but still feel empty inside.

Even worse, the Western world <u>is a society based on consumerism</u>, and the way of thought and behavior that discipline requires is often *disrupted* and *complicated* by this consumerist drive.

In fact, the western world is more than just a consumer society, it's a consumer culture, meaning that if you live here, you're surrounded by a value system (a "social contract" if you will) of consumerism as both heritage and societal custom. It's a way of life that encompasses literally every aspect of your existence which, in your attempts to build discipline, you need to understand.

When a country has a consumer culture, that doesn't just mean the people who live there excessively shop and consume, <u>it means that they communicate and find *personal meaning* through the act of consumption as well</u>. Consumerism isn't just about what people do with their spare time or disposable income; it's about what the infrastructure of such a hyper-commercialized society does to the *psyche* of such people as they become acclimated to it.[5]

In a consumer culture, as soon as you walk out of your door or turn on your television (and, in the upcoming future, as soon as you start your computer or even make a phone call) virtually everything you come across is designed to separate you from your money, not just by selling you products, but again, **by selling you products *as substitutions* for emotional and psychological needs.**

In essence, a commercialized society subliminally trains its inhabitants to believe that mere *products* can:

- define their identity (help them come across as cool, smart, sophisticated or socially conscious)

- resolve their anxieties (raise their attraction and desirability, or gain peer-validation) and

- find personal fulfillment (become a better mother, make an impact on the world,[6] etc.)

---

[5] American society is of course the primary example, but as the world becomes increasingly globalized and interconnected, similar patterns of thought and behavior are catching hold in even remote parts of the world (many Caribbean and East Asian countries, for instance). As Peter Finch's character proclaimed in the movie *Network*, "We're witnessing the death of the individual....America isn't the only place this is happening, we're just the most advanced nation so **we're getting there first**."

[6] This is what's referred to as "moral licensing" or "self-licensing."

...and the marketing that convinces them to do so - to use commercial products as a way to meet their inherent, human needs - *is based on instant-gratification*; an instant-gratification *neurosis* that undermines the principles of discipline so far described.

Since at least the 1950's (over half a century ago, mind you) advertising agencies began hiring professional psychologists to help devise their marketing methods. These psychologists, psychotherapists and social scientists were payed handsomely to discover how advertisements could latch onto deeper aspects of the human mind in order to convert more middle-class, relatively affluent Americans into paying customers: in order to convert what most people once saw as useless knick-knacks and luxuries into, instead, the newest, fascinating technological advancements they each "needed" to gain hold in the world.

This was initially referred to as the "depth approach," or motivational-analysis, style of marketing, in which, for instance:

  - *Soap* is positioned as a path to *beauty*

  - *Shoes* are positioned as a path to *lovely feet*

  - *Home appliance*s as a path to *good mothering* and of course

  - *Automobiles* a path to *prestige*.

So for instance, researchers found that women would pay up to *two dollars and half* for "skin cream" but no more than just twenty-five cents for "soap," because soap only promises to make one clean, whereas "skin cream" promises to make one beautiful. Once researchers found the motivational trigger was, the promise of beauty, "beauty products" began promising and masquerading themselves as such.

Likewise, when washing machines and microwaves were first sold to the public, most stay-at-home housewives viewed them as unnecessary; they were well-capable of those tasks as it were by themselves. Rather than stress the technical advantages of the machinery, therefore - the heating power of a microwave or load-capacity of a laundering machine, for instance - <u>marketers began to stress how home appliances make women a better mothers</u>, simply because the time a woman saved by using these new appliances could then be spent with her children, rather than on chores.

To this day even, when an old roommate of mine suggested I get a tattoo and I asked in return, *"What for?"* he said, *"To show your personality."*

I simply replied, *"Well, I have my personality to do that..."*

Of course, this is not an indictment against skin cream, microwaves, washing machines or tattoos. What I'm getting at here is that **you can't find happiness or personal fulfillment in objects the same way you can in your crafts, skills, talents, discipline and sense of self-mastery**; that you can't let the Western world tell you how to define yourself, nor let your creative impulse come to be contrived or contorted by the materialistic, consumerist thrust of our modern-day world.

REFERENCES AND FURTHER CONCERNS...

For more on discipline as the desire for mastery, see George Leonard's *Mastery: Keys to Success & Long-Term Fulfillment* or Thomas Sterner's *The Practicing Mind: Developing Focus & Discipline in Life.* Both titles detail, rather thoroughly, how one can master any skill or challenge by learning to love the process.

For more on our consumer-based, instant-gratification-oriented culture, see Vance Packard's *The Hidden Persuaders* (mentioned earlier) or *Four Arguments for the Elimination of Television* by Jerry Mander. Both titles give well-researched, accurate depictions about the nature of an advertisement-centric society and how such a society undermines and inhibits the discipline, and many other, more societal benefits, that result from process-oriented thinking.

Again, one attains discipline by valuing the refinement and craftsmanship of his creative skill *over and above* the success or material gain it may eventually come to produce. Keep this perspective in the forefront of your mind by remembering that:

- discipline, in the general sense, generally requires *a* discipline, in the specific sense, to sustain and exhibit itself through

- the results we get are rarely, if ever, directly proportional to the amount of time, energy or money we invest in order to obtain them (though we tend to assume this as the case) *until much later in the process,* and that

- you're attempting to become disciplined in an *anti-*discipline world

…because Western society conditions us to have a surface-level, consumerist and materialistic concept of existence that's *antagonistic* to the very nature of self-discipline in the first place.

Take a break to reflect and let's continue…

CH. 4: HOW TO BUILD MOTIVATION

"MOTIVATION IS BUILT INTERNALLY, FROM ONE'S SENSE OF IDENTITY; IT CAN NEVER BE DERIVED FROM AN EXTERNAL POINT OF REFERENCE..."

"Unhappy are those who attempt to win battles and succeed in their attacks without first cultivating the spirit of enterprise; the result is a waste of time and general stagnation." ~ Sun Tzu

"The lust for comfort kills the passion of the soul."
~ Khalil Gibran

Chapter 4 marks the halfway point of this book, an intermission if you will, primarily because everything prior involved mindset shifts based on perspective, whereas everything henceforth involves tactics based on actual behavior (rather than principles to understand). Before transitioning into this more practical sphere however, we'll cover two key ideas: first, that <u>75% of motivation is non-motivational</u>, and second, that you should <u>"be the Sun, not the planet."</u> Here's more...

75% OF MOTIVATION IS NON-MOTIVATIONAL

Just as 75% of communication is non-verbal - just as most of what you communicate can be found in your body language, tone of voice and the situation, or context, you say it within - rather than simply the words themselves, *75% of motivation is <u>non-motivational</u>* as well: most of how motivated you are can be found in your perspective towards life, your habitual behaviors and the people you associate with, rather than simply what you do, or fail to do, in order to "motivate" yourself.

Motivation, a lot like willpower, builds itself *indirectly*, as a response to factors that seem *unrelated* to it, and **these factors have more to do with your *identity* than they do with your source of inspiration or encouragement.**

When it comes to long-term motivation, you can't encourage, force or logically convince yourself to be, or stay, focused any more then you can encourage, force or logically convince someone to be, or stay, with you romantically. Long-term motivation is a type of "chemistry" which happens on its own accord, *as an offset to the type of person you are* and *consequential* to the type of life you choose to lead.

You can only build motivation, therefore, *by reverse-engineering it*; by building it into your character and into your subconscious thought process.

Again, just as 75% of communication is non-verbal, 75% of motivation is non-motivational, and <u>that 75% is internal, subtle and unconscious</u>. You can't gain long-term motivation by merely watching an inspirational movie, reading a New York Times Bestseller or placing affirmations on your bedroom wall, because the mere consumption of information (or the mere replication of mechanical routine) *is not* enough, by itself, to translate into a persistent sense of drive and ambition...these things have to be derived from within the depths of your own psyche and intuitive nature.

Don't get me wrong: books, movies, quotes and tactics of that sort are a great place to start, but long-term motivation begins with *re*-thinking and *re*-considering the deeper aspects of life we tend to leave on auto-pilot, or wholeheartedly ignore. For example:

- **Do you know your purpose in life?** Because without a clear sense of purpose, it's difficult to have a clear sense of order and direction, and without a clear sense of order and direction, *it's difficult to feel as though anything is worth the effort;* hence, difficult to remain motivated. You can't be motivated to act without purpose in life any more than you'd be motivated to hop on a subway train without an event or end-destination in mind, and that's why *people who manage their time well and remain focused tend to orient their careers and talents around a calling that drives them.*[1]

- **Do you know, and capitalize off of, your unique talents and strengths?** Because a goal that revolves around natural skill is far more conducive to superior performance (and superior results) than a goal that revolves around menial labor or the monotony of a resented task, as a goal that revolves around natural skill creates a feedback loop that amplifies into even more ambition to begin with. So although most people tend to focus on weakness - most try to compensate for what they're poor at and make up for what they don't have - *motivated people, conversely, tend to focus on strength, and by capitalizing off of their natural, unique talents and skills, their entire work-process becomes more optimistic, energizing, and motivating as well.*

- **Do you know, and tailor your life towards, your own personal values?** Because a man who follows a sense of principle and internal code, rather than just the social norms and expectations others pressure him to have, will develop a sense of personal dignity and self-empowerment, rather than hypocrisy and fraud which is, unfortunately, the operating system most prevalent in today's world. People who feel a zest and hunger for life tend to also think and behave in ways that reflect what they're truly about, and *they find courage to do so by overcoming their need for social acceptance and peer-validation.*

The idea here is that <u>long-term, external motivation rests upon a certain level of deep-rooted, internal strength</u>: that it can't exist without a certain level of emotional stability, mental poise, self-definition and other rare character traits which seem to be on the verge of extinction.

Once you start to consider motivation as this more durable, internal, "motive" power, not mere inspiration or encouragement, <u>you'll also begin to diagnose your lack of motivation at a higher plateau</u>: as a by-product of how you feel about the world, your place within it and your capacity to

---

[1] See David Deida's *The Way of the Superior Man* for more. As he says, "Without a conscious life purpose, <u>a man is totally lost</u>, drifting and adapting to events rather then creating them…without knowing his purpose, a man lives a weakened, impotent existence, perhaps even becoming sexually impotent, or prone to mechanical, disinterested sex."

fulfill that role, for example. In this way, building motivation, like attaining discipline, then becomes a matter of building character, or building one's self.

It's for this reason that motivation is constructed internally, from one's sense of identity, and can never be derived from an external point of reference.

Again, just as 75% of communication is non-verbal, 75% of motivation is *non-motivational*: most of it's determined by factors we'd rarely associate with our sense of ambition; very little by what we commonly do to "get motivated," find inspiration or encourage ourselves. Specifically...

- knowing your purpose in life

- developing your unique talents and skills towards that aim and

- adhering to your higher sense of personal code

...are key factors to this overall concern. Let's now cover the frame of mind most favorable towards this approach.

BE THE SUN, NOT THE PLANET

To "be the Sun, not the planet," simply means to **take responsibility for your life by defining it, and living it, on your own terms.** As a metaphor, just as the Sun is a central, radiant force that *maintains its position*, unlike planets, which orbit around another celestial body, you yourself should be a central, radiant force who *maintains their ground*, unlike most people, who merely orbit around another person's *game plan* or manner of existence.

This doesn't mean to have an egotistical, narcissistic attitude or to think of yourself as the center of the world, but to ensure that the "solar system" of your life reflects and honors your own personal code and ensues on your own personal terms and best interests.

Knowing your life purpose, developing your unique talents and defining your personal values are the main ways to do this, but as you begin to blend this mentality into your overall conduct, you'll see its implications in a variety of other ways.

For instance, another way you can be the sun is by <u>defining success for yourself and by being successful in your own way</u>, which is far more rewarding (and a lot easier, actually) then pursuing some career path others have laid out for you.

Don't let the less-talented or less-daring discourage you from your goals, or convince you they're senseless. Don't let a parent, wife, husband, group of friends or anyone else incarcerate you to their perspective of what your life should become, because *you're* the one who has to live it and deal with the consequences your decisions entail.

Don't be a follower: don't rotate around others who don't embody your personal vision of progress and wellbeing. Learn to be selfish in a healthy way by...

- drawing clear boundaries between yourself and the parasites trying to drain you

- accepting that you *won't* be accepted for your individuality and

- remembering that since you're unique, you won't be able to bring *all* of your friends with you into the future you're going to establish.

Also, similarly, <u>set goals for yourself based on the reality of your actual, current situation</u>, rather than in comparison to some starry-eyed, mythical ideal. Remember the graphs from the last chapter; pace yourself for progress in relation to your present standing, and never allow yourself to feel intimidated, because you're in competition with no one but yourself.

It's difficult to build motivation and get engaged when your goals are based on external cues or social validation; at some level, you'll know that to be nothing but mimicry and imitation. It's also difficult to build motivation and get engaged when you're constantly comparing yourself to unrealistic measures of success; at some level, you'll know that to be practically impossible.

Lastly, a third way to be the sun is on a more emotional front, by <u>never allowing another person, or circumstance, to dictate your temperament</u> or state of mind. To a certain extent, whenever you let someone's ignorance or disrespect get the best of you, *you also let that person control you*, and whenever you grow distraught over temporary failure (or situations which you can't control) you, for at least that time being, have a victim mentality.

As a general rule, the more dramatic and emotional you react to a negative event, the more likely you'll regress backwards into childhood patterns of behavior and thought, whereas the more calm and composed you remain, the more deliberately you can tailor how you feel and behave to whatever a situation demands. So do your best to keep a calm, composed demeanor at all times, and effect a cool disposition.

Don't let circumstances define your identity for you: don't let financial troubles, a failed romance or any other setback puppeteer you into who you're going to be. We all face pain in life, so it's natural to be down at times, but ultimately, you have to make a conscious *choice* about the type of person you are, and maintain that stance regardless of what occurs or what other people do to you, otherwise your motivation will come to be less reliable than the weather. [2]

Remember *that things come and go*. You could have a great corporate job and lose it overnight because of an executive scandal, or some white-collar crime that leads the firm into bankruptcy. You could have a perfect partner who suddenly becomes a drug addict, loses their sanity or simply leaves you for someone half your age or double your income, and so on. As we spoke of in the last chapter, just as you can't find happiness, or internal strength, through commercial products, you can't find happiness, or internal strength, through ideal circumstances either. Remember this…

Again, motivation is built internally, from one's sense of identity; it's can never derived from an external point of reference. Thus a good metaphor to keep in mind is "be the Sun, not the planet" meaning to conscientiously set up a solar-system that reflects your own personal values and unique definitions for success.

REFERENCES AND FURTHER CONCERNS…

Ayn Rand's body of work - novels such as *Atlas Shrugged* and *The Fountainhead* or short plays such as "Ideal" and "Night of January 16th" - articulate the substance, ethos and convictions this chapter hopes to convey better than any other writing I've come across. There's a distinct style of thinking, both a distinct philosophical approach towards human interaction and towards one's own creative power; Rand's literature is known world-over for depicting with eloquent prose. In her own words:

"The man who thinks must think and act on his own. A reasoning mind cannot work under any form of compulsion - it cannot be subordinated to the needs, opinions or wishes of others, because it is not an object of sacrifice."

---

[2] Syrian writer Publilius Syrus says, "Depend on conduct, not fortune."; that "Anyone can hold the helm while the sea is calm."

"Man's proper state is an upright posture, an intransigent mind and a step that travels unlimited roads…"

For more on discovering your life's purpose (and the internal strength needed to pursue it), see David Deida's *The Way of the Superior Man,* Marcia Power's *The Dragon Slayer with a Heavy Heart,* Richard Bach's *Jonathan Livingston Seagull* or Wallace Wattles's *The Science of Being Great.* Of all these, Wattles's work is the most technical and straightforward; Power's the most passionate and moving.

With these key understandings laid out, that:

1. to conquer yourself is to be at tactical war with both your biological instincts and your social conditioning, simultaneously, that

2. procrastination begins by confusing what you're able to accomplish with what your personal value is as a human being, that

3. we're most disciplined when we aim to master a skill, not collect a reward and that

4. motivation is built internally, from one's sense of identity, and can never be derived from an external reference

…let's now move into a more strategic, technical course of action. Take a break to reflect and continue at your own pace.

CH.5: HOW TO RAISE PRODUCTIVITY

"PRODUCTIVITY IS THE NATURAL OUTGROWTH
OF FOCUS, CLARITY AND CONCENTRATION."

"Beyond the noble art of getting things done lies the noble art of leaving things undone. The wisdom of life resides in the elimination of nonessentials."
~ Lin Yutang

"Our entire world is suffering from a chronic case of attention deficit disorder."
~ Rich Schefren

OUR ENTIRE WORLD SUFFERS FROM ATTENTION-DEFICIT DISORDER

In an age where we've come to depend on mass-scale, instant-communication technology (high-speed wifi internet networks, SMS text-messaging, tablet computing and so forth) the average person's ability to concentrate has atrophied beyond repair; as we enjoy our world of constant digital connectivity, *we pay for it with the severe price of constant inattentiveness as well.*

In fact, China, Taiwan and Korea have recently accepted "Internet Addiction Disorder" (IAD) *as a psychiatric diagnosis,* and this year IAD was just added to the American DSM-V - the "Diagnostic and Statistical Manual of Mental Disorders" (Fifth Edition), as well.

We're losing our ability to focus, which is **the same ability that allows us to be productive and goal-oriented to begin with**. So although technology is far too integrated into business, education and overall society to function without, it's also shortening our attention-spans and gradually alienating us from even knowing what it means to concentrate at all. Such grave absence of concentration is what keeps us from…

  - refining our talents into skills

  - using our brains to think clearly

  - making good, split-second decisions, and

  - doing the in-depth, long-term work we need in order to obtain results

As an analogy, the reason why a knife can cut, whereas a spoon or fork can't, is because the blade of a knife is designed in a way which focuses the entire force of one's hand towards a specific point, not several points simultaneously as the fork does, or a smooth general surface with no point at all, as the spoon.

Similarly, the reason a laser can cut, a hammer can drive nails, an actor can memorize lines, a student can master new subjects and a dancer can learn new routines is because *they're all utilizing focused energy in a concentrated direction*; because they're all doing <u>the opposite</u> of the attention-deficiency syndrome our hyper-robotic civilization is gearing you towards.

No different than a laser or knife, there's only so much energy you can direct towards a specific point or objective. The amount of productivity you achieve is regulated by how deeply you penetrate into that aim.

While you probably don't have only a single goal to accomplish, *have, as an ideal, a work-style resembling a blade in that it accomplishes only singular tasks in succession*, because this single-mindedness is what'll convert your efforts into large-order results.

To raise your productivity, treat single-mindedness as the only sensible approach to possess, and personally engineer ways to sustain it over gradually longer periods of time, because the amount of "work" you complete is an offset to the degree of concentration you maintain while working.

In a second, we'll discuss how to build concentration exactly - not by practicing memorization exercises or training your attention span deliberately, but by modifying the technological habits that tend to dominate modern-day life. But remember, *our entire society is suffering from a chronic case of attention deficit disorder*: take a careful look around you to see how our overflow of gadgetry and digital contraptions, while providing *the delusion* of enhanced productivity, ironically serve to sabotage it instead.

First however, let's talk about "time-management" in both traditional and twenty-first century terms...

TIME-MANAGEMENT IS "PLAYED OUT"

Because our world suffers from attention-deficit - because there's an inordinate amount of technology making attention-deficit disorder the norm rather than the exception - *traditional time-management is played out*. In our modern, digital age, **traditional time-management techniques no longer suffice, because traditional time-management stems from a society which no longer exists**.

The phrase "time management" originally dates back to the Industrial Revolution, from about 1760-1840: *the first time in human history in which "output" or "production" for the average worker could exceed the boundaries of nature.* So whereas in a previous, agrarian economy…

- the type of work one did was determined by the seasons or landscape he lived in, or upon

- the hours of work he held was determined simply by the hours of sunlight he had available,

- the holidays he took off by inclement weather and

- even time itself by a mere glance up at the Sun and Moon

…the Industrial Revolution was the first epoch in human history where man began to use clocks, work in factories, travel long distances (with trains), manufacture goods rather than hand-produce them and leave his rural hometown to pursue opportunity in major, metropolitan cities.

Most time-management literature and related concepts came slightly later of course, but still have their philosophical origin in a time in where there was *no* internet, *no* cell phones, *no* fax machines and no such thing as "technology" in the sense we think of today - in the sense which in fact literally *governs* how we work, interact and communicate now.

As opposed to time-management then, a more apt term would be "attention management" or what's academically referred to as <u>attention-economics</u>: techniques for personal and professional effectiveness that regard *attention* as our most precious resource in today's digital age rather than mere time.

Thinking in terms of attention is far more congruent with today's social environment, **but it's also far more counter-intuitive.** The rest of this chapter will describe methods to raise it, but keep in mind that the overall aim is to shelter your attention from the technological influences now dissipating and squandering it; that **the key to productivity, more than any other single factor, is simply focus, clarity and concentration.**

Again, *traditional time-management played out.* This isn't to suggest the spirit or essence of time-management to be no longer of use, but that the techniques emerged during a former phase of human activity, and so the specific skills should be seen only as a composite or subset of the larger, more modern and suitable concern of *attention* instead.

The reality is that you can't even manage time[1], you can only manage yourself, and the aspect of yourself most applicable to output and productivity, in today's world, is your ability to focus - your capacity to concentrate and hone in on, single-mindedly, the specific tasks most pivotal to your progress and creative success.

So eliminate the word "time management" from your vocabulary and substitute it with terms like "productivity," and "efficiency" as an alternative. Substitute the focus on day-planners, agendas, smartphone applications and to-do lists with a focus on the following procedures…

PRINCIPLE #1: ELIMINATE DISTRACTION

Jay-Z once said, *"Sometimes I don't even stop to give people autographs, because if I were to do that, I'd never get where I'm going,"* which, metaphorically, is a wise attitude to embrace, because if you stop to "sign autographs" (as in, address every upcoming concern), you'll never "get where you're going" (as in, where your aspirations require you to be) either.

He said this on a documentary covering *The Hard-Knock Life Tour* in 1999, which was, again, before social networks and pervasive cell-phone use even existed. With today's influx of web-technology, we've each become like miniature celebrities in our own right, and so we each have to manage our own share of distraction, interruption, endless correspondence and lack of privacy as well.

If you get nothing else from this chapter, remember that **while the amount of time and energy you have is finite, the amount of *demands* being placed on your time and energy are virtually infinite**…there's literally no end to how much people can ask of you, intrude on you or otherwise subtract and deduct from your ability to focus. This being so, the first key principle for raising productivity, particularly when it comes to creative work, is to eliminate distraction; to simply *stop allowing* yourself to be distracted.

---

[1] You can't manage time because the word "manage" essentially means to control, and no matter what you do, there's only twenty-four hours in a day, seven days in a week and 365 days in a year. In actuality therefore, though you may think this pure semantics, time isn't an uncontrollable characteristic of nature which can never be managed at all.

Once you have a specific task or objective in mind, stop letting random, trivial interruptions prevent you from doing it, because <u>distraction and interruption rob us of more productivity than just about any other single factor</u>.

Distractions not only take you off track and disturb your train of thought, they take you *so* off track that it'll typically require two to three-times as long to establish the original concentration you had before you were disturbed to begin with, which, again, is simply assassination for anything artistic.

Even further, distraction not only prevents you from getting important things done within a reasonable space of time; it can also, very easily, become a habitual pattern of behavior that leaves you incapable of accomplishing anything significant whatsoever.

Seriously, take some to reflect on this and you'll realize that *every time you allow yourself to be interrupted by a trivial concern, you actually pay for that interruption <u>with a piece of your future</u>*. In a sense, every meaningless distraction, every tweet, IM message and email notice, is "purchased" by sacrificing a small fragment of your most significant goal, in the same way your long-term wealth is sacrificed with every insignificant purchase and impulse buy.

You need to focus, so learn to set up an environment that allows you to systematically shut out distraction and interruption at will. Once it's time to get started…

- turn off your email alerts and social network notifications

- sign out of Facebook and Skype

- put your cellphone on mute

- let the important people in your life know you won't be available for a certain period of time (or wake up much earlier than they do)

- physically leave the places you normally occupy (libraries and coffee shops are great for this)

…and so on. Always minimize the effect of interruptions by keeping them brief of course, but don't stop there: whenever you find yourself getting distracted from your work, by anything, *engineer a way to systematically prevent that distraction from ever happening again*. Always think about how you can set up *a creative environment* or artistic space that naturally shelters your attention span for you; that allows you to focus and concentrate without conscientiously attempting to do so.

For instance, for your Facebook account, <u>set a bookmark for your profile page rather than the normal, public news-feed</u> and for your email account, <u>bookmark your actual inbox rather than the more commercial, news-oriented homepage</u>. This way you won't get distracted by the random events, pointless gossip or any of the other attention-wasting dynamics that literally flood and dominate these sites.[2]

Instead, if you set your bookmarks up in this way, you'll be immediately sent to the window specified for what you had in mind to do only; you'll be anchored to the actual "productivity" of the webpage rather than loosely floating throughout it.

Similarly, <u>set up specific time-windows for correspondence</u> where you'll return phone calls and reply to email. Interestingly, you'll find that you can actually train and condition people to expect a response from you only during the range of hours which complement your schedule instead of impede it. They'll unconsciously come to realize that you return calls only in the evening or only in the morning, and eventually accommodate their needs to that routine.

This may seem selfish, but conversely, if you do the opposite of that, if you *always* pick up your phone and *always* reply to emails as soon as you get them, you'll send the opposite message: underneath the convenience of your availability will be the subtle idea, *"Hey you know, you can bother and interrupt me at any time you want. It's okay, my life is pretty much yours to respond to, so whenever you get the whim, just pick up the phone and dial me. I'll be your personal fire-fighter, no problem."*

Remember, **while your time, energy and attention span are all finite, the demands being placed on (and requests being made for) your time, energy and attention span are virtually infinite.** There'll *always* be someone who:

- "needs" your help for their "emergency"

- wants you to join their humanitarian cause for "social justice"

---

[2] Many websites are structurally designed to grab your attention (as in, *steal it*) as this how they generate ad-revenue.

- support their multi-level marketing campaign for "financial freedom"

- just sell you their cheap products or, even worse

- just dump their latest negativity and drama onto you

...so until you begin to treat this as mostly noise - until you begin to establish boundaries, stop firefighting other people's issues, proactively set the frame of activity for yourself and shelter your goals from invasion - your day-to-day productivity will always falter, your projects will always sit on the fence and your goals will always slide into the background for somebody else's momentary impulse. You may even come to hold a slight sense of resentment because of it.

So do whatever it takes to eliminate distraction and interruption at will, as much as you humanly can, and make that process entirely systematic. Make the elimination of distraction so fundamental to how your work is structured that you no longer have to even consider it. When it's time to work, turn off everything, sign out of everything, set up the technology you need to use so it's as honed as it possibly can be and physically leave your normal places of occupancy.[3]

If it helps, simply think of distraction and interruption as computer viruses or religious sins you're obligated to avoid at all costs, and then strategize ways to safeguard yourself from them.

PRINCIPLE #2: STOP MULTITASKING

It's been said that *multitasking decreases your IQ more than smoking marijuana*, and while this isn't *technically* true, as it decreases your IQ only *during* the time your multitasking, not permanently like drugs do, the concept still touches on a point worth exploring here.[4]

---

[3] In extreme cases, like mine, you may have to set up a situation where *people don't even know where you are.*

[4] If you're in the habit of relying on marijuana, or any drug really, to be creative, productive or stable in any sense of the word (emotionally, psychologically, etc.), my opinion is that you're probably on the verge of something disastrous - on the verge of a dependency syndrome that needs to be addressed immediately, if not sooner. Take time to think this over, carefully.

<u>Multitasking, contrary to popular opinion, is not productive…it's _counter_-productive</u>: rather than build your personal efficiency, it actually detracts from it, so _in order_ to become more efficient, <u>stop doing it</u>. While there are times during the day where we're all forced to multitask, as discussed, our devices have brought us to a point where we're simply multitasking all the time; it's another destructive habit crippling our ability to focus and obtain results.

The very same tools that allow others to distract us also allow us to distract ourselves, but since that behavior tends to hide under the deceptive cloak of "multitasking," it's a discrepancy that goes largely unnoticed. Since we're constantly being distracted, it's as though we're constantly trying to make up for that by doing more than one thing at a time…a habit which, ironically, leaves us accomplishing not much at all.

The more common idea, the notion that multitasking makes us more productive (not less), is a cultural myth, and a quick online search for "studies on multitasking" reveals why. **Multitasking, and electronic multitasking specifically, temporarily reduces our intellectual capacity**: it decreases our ability to concentrate, solve problems and think creatively, while also increasing stress levels and hampering our ability to communicate and remain aware of the environment which surrounds us. For instance:

- If you're trying to type out an email while you're also on the phone with someone, you're not going to be as effective building the connection or negotiating in either endeavor. You may even end up saying something you can't take back or emailing the wrong person.

- If you're writing a report and doing internet research _for_ the report simultaneously (two activities that appear to be one and the same), the research will eventually distract you from the writing. You'll end up following links to completely unrelated information, social networking and heading down a spiral of useless activities that lead nowhere while still leaving you drained.

- You may even have what's referred to as "tab-itis," the mock internet-born illness of feeling compelled to always have nine, ten, fifteen or even twenty webpages open in different tabs all at once. What's interesting here is that usually once you're finally done and ready to turn off your computer, you'll still have nine, ten fifteen or even twenty webpages open which you "haven't finished looking at yet."

In my case, my biggest blunder here was *multitasking writing with work.* No man can serve two masters of course, but I tried, many times, for weeks on end actually, to serve as both a writer and an office manager at the same time.

During tax season, I help prepare returns out of a small office here in Queens, so last year, whenever I wasn't busy processing paperwork, I'd sneak a few minutes away to process this book instead. Since I was already past deadline, multitasking was meant, ironically, as a strategy to help finish the book faster: so instead of answering phone calls to address a taxpayer's concerns, I spent every free moment I could gather editing sections, reformatting outlines and so on.

How did this method prove? *Disastrous*, to say the least...

With the writing, naturally, my flow was continuously broken: I couldn't write or edit anything without having to answer the door, return a phone call or be otherwise interrupted ("interrupted" *at* work *by* the very same work I was being paid to perform, mind you). I'd thus continuously lose the momentum of a transitional paragraph, the phrasing of a critical sentence or, in many cases, an entire concept itself.

With the tax work though, interestingly, I grew impatient and began rushing our clientele. I began to seeing them not as honest, taxpaying citizens who simply needed my help, but *as distractions* blockading me from my most meaningful goal.

This was doubly deceptive because, as you may know, Income Tax preparation is a paperwork -oriented business: almost *none* of it can be done over the phone. Since most of the phone calls were based either on ignorance or laziness though, not proper tax work itself, I felt like the type of calls I had to answer *verified* and *validated* my neglectful approach rather then expose it for what it was.

An emotional tinge of frustration began to subtly paint over **both** the tax work and the literary process. I was frustrated at the phone calls and the people that came in for disrupting me, and then also frustrated at myself for being seemingly incapable of editing a manuscript that was already late, already promised and already *pre-ordered*…already sold to clients and friends who believed in me and patiently exhibited faith in that which had yet to even exist.

I'd be on the phone with a taxpayer thinking to myself, *"Damn, this person again? Why won't they write their estimate down somewhere so they'll remember it? Why do they keep losing their 1040 and W-2's?"*

And just a few minutes later, I'd be editing a chapter of the book thinking to myself, *"Damn, why do these people keep interrupting me? See??? Forgot what I was going to say again."*

My Father was the one who finally talked me out of it. It seems obvious now, but it wasn't until someone *told me* that I needed to dedicate myself and my conscientiousness *entirely* to work when I was at work and *entirely* to writing when I was writing - that I simply needed come into the office a couple hours earlier to ensure such dedication- when anything began to take shape; *that's* when I was finally able to address customers with the focus and attention they deserved *and* write this manual with clarity and concentration it requires.

Note how <u>multitasking put me an emotional state *inconsistent* with what all creative work characteristically demands</u>; how multitasking wasn't just a material hindrance, and how, even if I didn't *sound* like I was being disrupted (which I probably did) and even beyond the fact that I wasn't psychologically "there" with a client enough to properly resolve their concerns, <u>the inhibited productivity cascaded upon itself</u>; multitasking caused me to lose my composure and lose the internal sense of stability that intelligence needs in order to express itself; that one's imagination literally yearns for in order to come forward.

When you're doing creative work, or *any* work that requires active thinking and decision making, you need to be able to check in with yourself; to have a level of metacognition and self-awareness that can say, *"Something's wrong here…I'm not on-point right now,"* or *"I need to take a break."* However, to have this metacognition, you first have to circumvent the habits and tendencies preventing you from obtaining it, particularly the same multitasking that'll, instead, nudge you towards the flustered state I was in since, as a society, we unintentionally, and mistakenly, consider multitasking to be a productivity enhancer.

As discussed earlier, there *are* times and situations when you need to multitask, because our modern world forces us to. But in order to raise your productivity, it's best to limit this as much as you humanly can. Restrict multitasking to whatever *doesn't* require creativity or thinking (mechanical tasks like cleaning, dishwashing, exercising and so on); behaviors that are routine, unconscious or domestic, but *never* creative, experimental or concentration-entailed.

Remember, no man can serve two masters, and no creative thinker can productively conquer two tasks at once either.

The worse part about multitasking isn't simply that it inhibits your productivity, but that <u>it leaves you incapable of developing skill</u>. Recall that in order to attain discipline and turn your talents into strengths, you need to concentrate on refining the particular dynamics those talents and strengths are composed of. That is, to gain mastery at something, you have to go in-depth and first master the minute details and aspects of that particular thing, but you'll never get around to doing that if you're too busy multitasking.

It's a rather profound concern actually, because:

- even when we go to sleep, rather than just lie there and concentrate on getting a good night's rest, we worry about what we're going to do tomorrow or review something negative from the day and

- even when we're talking to someone, rather than just listen and concentrate on what that person is saying, we calculate our next response or daydream of something completely unrelated, etc. etc.

So even when we're not <u>apparently</u> multitasking, we're usually <u>psychologically</u> multitasking instead; going through a mere mental extension of the same phenomenon, and this "parallel processing" diminishes not only our productivity, but our ability to extract value and meaning out of <u>everything</u> we experience.

The more you have going on, the more you compound this problem, so practice focusing on one task at a time and exercise your ability to concentrate thoroughly. Whenever you catch yourself multitasking, *stop* and remind yourself to go deep into the specific activity you originally set out to do.

Take a break to reflect and let's continue…

PRINCIPLE #3: DISREGARD THE NONESSENTIAL

Likewise, to further sustain your concentration and clarity, don't just stop at eliminating distraction and refusing to multitask, **disregard the nonessential as well;** raise your productivity higher by learning to:

- disregard all unproductive busywork (whatever ties up your time without drawing you closer towards your goals)

- delegate as much as you can, *whenever* you can

- ask for help when it's necessary and

- reserve the right to say "no" when someone asks you to join their cause, take on their responsibilities or firefight their personal problems

...because before you can break your goals down into smaller, easier-to-conquer phases and routines (more on this later), you have to first <u>drop some of your goals completely</u>.

As the Chinese inventor Lin Yutang once said, *"Beyond getting things done lies the noble art of leaving things undone. The wisdom of life resides in the elimination of nonessentials."* Life is full of responsibilities and obligations, but your productivity won't excel without conscientiousness as to the responsibilities and obligations you've unnecessarily nominated yourself *for*, nor without the courage to disregard and gradually phase yourself away from those concerns.

Your productivity won't excel until you're able to call people you've already committed to and say *"Look, I've been doing some thinking, and with everything going on* (at graduate school, with my daughter, with my upcoming screenplay, etc.), *I don't think I'm going to be able to* (meet with the club, carry out administrative duties, so on and so forth) *any longer."*[5]

Your productivity won't fully excel, of course, until you're able to <u>preemptively</u> know when someone's asking you to take on too much - until you're able to <u>intuitively</u> sense when you're getting in over your head - but, as it stands now, if you're like most people, you *already* need to

---

[5] You'll find, surprisingly, that most people are far more considerate and understanding towards your personal situation than you'd expect. As long as you're respectful and up-front about things, rather than shirk responsibilities you claimed you could handle, they'll appreciate the honesty and the communication more than anything else; probably too impressed with your character to even notice.

terminate certain contracts and commitments in order to simply have the free time and space your creative work demands of you.

Remember: **none of us are made of bubblegum; we can each only stretch so thin.** And again, although life is full of responsibilities and obligations, your productivity won't excel without conscientiousness as to the responsibilities and obligations you've unnecessarily nominated yourself for, nor without the courage to disregard and gradually phase yourself away from those concerns.

Besides other people and organizations, keep in mind that much of your own personal behavior, albeit goal-related, may also fall into the category of nonessential as well, no different, and perhaps even more so, than what your associates ask of you. Just because *you* decided to do something doesn't mean that it's a productive thing to do, so *let go* of activities that:

- don't relate to actual progress

- don't convert themselves efficiently into results or

- no longer reflect the path you wish to travel in life

… just like you would any of the unnecessary obligations mentioned above.

For instance, most of the social networking, email correspondence, internet research and, honestly, almost *everything* I see people doing when pursuing a new goal is simply *a new distraction*: tasks that neither relate to their final aim nor force the individual towards any actual work itself.

I know a cinematographer who, before submitting her early college work to a local film festival, suggested doing "research" into getting licensing for her project's background music; as she didn't have permission to use any of the songs she did. She thought it a good idea to "look into" what copyright provisions her current level of filmmaking entails, so she could then follow that process exactly, "just to be safe."

"But it's not a commercial project," I said. "Just send it in and worry about it if, and after, anyone contacts you."

"What happens if I get <u>sued</u>???"

"Nobody's going to 'sue' you because you're not making any <u>money</u>. Even if someone did want to sue you, the legal expenses required to do so would make it counterproductive."

"Yeah, that's what everyone says until they end up <u>in the penitentiary</u>. I just want to protect myself."

"What are you talking about??? Nobody's going to lock you up for using a few jazz tunes in the background of what was initially a school project…a project you're not even selling. If anybody contacts you, just say you didn't know you couldn't use the songs for educational purposes, and that you'll remove the film from circulation until you change the background music."

This is just one example, but in it you can see how fear - the need for security, aversion to risk and so on - can inhibit your productivity just as much as any other distraction, because there'll always be <u>thousands</u> of nonessential things you should do in order to "protect yourself."

Just in case you're unsure, know that when it comes to being a creative professional, <u>safety doesn't exist</u>. There's nothing wrong with being meticulous, but if you're a one-man operation (like I and most other creative thinkers I know are), not some multi-national corporate entity, you mist <u>dedicate yourself and your energy to tasks that *generate revenue* and *produce results*</u>, not worry or nitpick over every possible danger. Just assume that there's risk involved with any endeavor you pursue, and cross that bridge when you get there.

Another interesting idea creative people seem to be fixated on is going to "business school," to supplement their creative talents with hardcore "entrepreneurial know-how."

Again, just in case you're unsure here too, know that *the education industry is exactly that: an industry,* as in a business, or, in layman's terms, *a hustle.* As a general rule, schooling is truly for people who have a specific career path in which they *need* the schooling in order to become properly licensed, trained and accredited *for,* or for young people who simply need an open space in order to find themselves and discover their identity. Anything other than that is usually just marketing, and there's a lot of unemployed twenty-something year-olds with over *$50,000* in debt, or more, to prove it.[6]

---

[6] Apparently, student-loan debt has now surpassed even credit-card debt as our nation's largest source of insolvency.

<u>You can't use schooling to teach you a fundamental life skill</u> or to supplant a weakness in your personality any more than you can use a couple hours in traffic school to teach you how to actually *drive*. In order to really learn something, you need to be in a *real* environment with *real* sacrifices, *real* expenses and *real* risks. Anything other than that is simply misguided, and anything other than that which *costs* top-dollar is simply good salesmanship.

So if you need business skills, get out there and learn business skills with *your own* money and *your own* reputation on the line. In many cases, the unproductive busy-work of online classes, term papers and so on is a long-winded, circuitous that may ultimately lead nowhere.

Again, **disregard the nonessential**: simply avoid and nullify the prospect of doing anything that doesn't lead to your actual progress. **The shortest distance between two points is always a straight line**, so always follow (and when necessary, go so far as to *invent*) the most efficient, streamlined process you conceivably can.

It's difficult to be disciplined or productive when you feel overwhelmed or submerged, so:

- develop the awareness to know when you're too inundated for your own good

- ask for help when you need it.[7]

- keep your work as streamlined and straightforward as possible and

- use your God-given right to say *no* in order to keep your schedule and life manageable

...because until you do, you'll jeopardize everything you have planned. Consider a task heavily once it's proposed to you - think of the steps involved, analyze how critical it is to the end result - and simplify the equation from there.[8]

---

[7] When it comes to delegation, the idea *"If you want something done right, you have to do it yourself,"* bears some truth to it, but we tend to take that too far: we tend to feel intimidated or ashamed asking for help with things we believe we should already know (getting a new wardrobe, learning to drive, etc.) Always remember that there's people willing to help; that it's not a good idea to try to do, or teach yourself, everything alone.

[8] Likewise, even when you're simply organizing your work space or a closet at home, a big part that organization isn't merely rearranging or categorizing your possessions, but *de-cluttering* and discarding the items which no longer serve you, as <u>the longer you hold onto your old stuff, *the longer you end up holding on to your old identity*</u>.

Remember, *none of us are bubblegum...we can only stretch so thin* and that *"beyond getting things done lies the noble art of leaving things undone"*; that *"the wisdom of life resides in the elimination of nonessentials."*

PRINCIPLE #4: CLOSE OPEN CIRCUITS

Technically speaking, an open circuit is an electrical system *with a gap in it,* causing the circuit to malfunction and the current to thus no longer flow. Metaphorically speaking however, here, **an open circuit is a piece of unfinished business** - a gap created by not finalizing what you began - which can then cause *your own plans* to malfunction by creating productivity-drainage or leakage in your "circuit" of affairs.

The habit of leaving circuits open, of...

- leaving issues unaddressed

- problems unsolved

- agreements unkept and

- obligations incomplete

...will undermine your productivity in hundreds of subtle, indiscreet ways, because the commitments we postpone tend to nag at our subconscious and dissipate our attention while the commitments we *completely ignore* tend to resurface in the future, drawing us away from our current objectives in life.

So even though the section prior stressed the exact opposite (disregarding the nonessential and letting things go) *there's a tendency here to act on either side of two extremes:* to either be an octopus who acts as though they have eight legs with which to do any and everything, or a total recluse who acts as though they can simply meditate their responsibilities out of existence, neglecting issues as if they'll resolve themselves *"Hakuna Matata"* style. This section speaks to the latter.

In essence, no matter what you do or who you become, <u>certain elements of your past will always remain with you,</u> and similarly, no matter how streamlined or focused your work-process may become, there'll always be minor, peripheral side-concerns which you're forced to address. So unless you want your burdens coming back to haunt you - anything random or trivial sabotaging your entire operation - get into the habit of fixing problems while they're still small, thinking long-term and of always being on-point.

Even race cars in the *Daytona 500* or hovercrafts in the video game *F-Zero* stop periodically to check their engines and maintain their vehicle, or maneuver around course obstacles and other competitors, so think of yourself and your ambitions in similar fashion: while productivity's about *accelerating* towards a single destination, that doesn't mean it's wise to exist in your own shell or simply avoid the outlying, tangential concerns of life (like your health, for instance).

Again, **close your open circuits**; always treat unfinished business with a laser-like quality of attention until it's completely resolved…

- If you feel a slight pain in your body, *don't ignore it until you're forced to go to the doctor*

- If you notice a negative habit in a group project or in a relationship, *don't neglect it because it's small*

- If you have a problem with someone you're required to be around, or someone you just care for and respect, talk to them about things honestly and officially square the issue away, so as to clear your mind of the concern

…etc. etc., because slight pains and small issues like these, left unaddressed, tend to amplify and accrue (like financial interest) until they become considerable pains and significant issues (like financial *debt*) that are difficult to take care of.

If you don't practice preemptive problem-solving, you'll be forced to practice reactionary damage-control, so take a second to think about the subtle threats that you're currently neglecting, which you truly know you can't delegate or avoid, and be productive in addressing them no different than your most meaningful aim.

Again, *don't let external obligations stack up on you; if you do, you'll soon become frozen and made stationary by the weight they compound.*

Whether you're conscious of it or not, open circuits create gaps in your mental clarity, demands on your physical energy and strains on your emotional poise, so make a conscious decision to bring each of your affairs to finality: either see issues through to the end or terminate your involvement altogether, but never let them dwindle or perpetuate indefinitely.

REFERENCES AND FURTHER CONCERNS...

Once more, **productivity is the natural outgrowth of focus, clarity and concentration**; you raise your productivity by either neutralizing the factors that impair concentration, or cultivating those that advance it. Principally, this includes the four principles of:

- creating a work environment that shelters your attention span by (1) *eliminating distraction*

- developing a work style that hones your efficiency by (2) *refusing to multitask*

- freeing up time and energy to focus by (3) *disregarding the nonessential* and

- bringing closure to your peripheral obligations by (4) *closing open circuits*

...so in the same way you build motivation by diagnosing how you feel about the world, you raise productivity by diagnosing how you behave when it's actually time to work; by examining how conducive your work process is to both singularity of both thought and proper allocation of activity.

But since our entire world suffers from attention-deficit disorder, and since traditional time-management techniques apply to a world that no longer exists, reinforce this new approach to productivity with Eben Pagan's video training series *Wake Up Productive*. For more on concentration specifically, see Scott Scheper's book How To Get Focused.

To learn more about multitasking as a counter-productive and inhibiting force rather than a constructive one, see The Myth of Multitasking: How "Doing it All" Gets Nothing Done by Dave Crenshaw, and for a more systematic discussion of email overload in particular - if this is a serious problem for you, but still an integral, necessary part of your daily life - see Merlin Mann's blog and website, InboxZero.com

For more on the perspective towards schooling discussed earlier (higher education as a financially impractical option for many people) see Dale J. Stephens's <u>Hacking Your Education: Ditch The Lectures, Save Tens of Thousands and Learn More Then Your Peers Ever Will</u>, or visit his website, <u>UnCollege.org</u>

Also, for an interesting read on how technology undermines not only our productivity, but also our relationships, sense of intimacy and human interaction as a whole, see <u>Alone Together: How We Expect More From Technology and Less From Each Other</u> by Sherry Turkle. In it, Turkle describes how although we assume technology is bringing us closer, simply because we're more connected to the world in a global sense, the reality is that it's making us *more* disconnected from the people who truly matter, including our very own selves.[9]

For a deeper review of the overall process of eliminating distraction, honing your ability to focus, disregarding the nonessential and this chapter as a whole, see Mark Joyner's book <u>Simpleology: The Simple Science of Getting Things Done</u>," or enjoy a free web-course of the same at his site <u>Simpleology.com</u>

Let's continue…

---

[9] Highly recommended.

CH. 6: HOW TO DEVELOP SYSTEMS

"YOU CAN'T ENHANCE OR REFINE AN ACTIVITY YOU DON'T
STATISTICALLY GAUGE OR SYSTEMATICALLY UNDERSTAND."

"Processes that are measured improve…processes that are
measured and then reported improve exponentially."
~ Eben Pagan

"I must create a system, or else live by another's."
~ William Blake

A SYSTEM IS LIKE A SKELETAL STRUCTURE

As you come to end procrastination, attain discipline, build motivation and raise productivity, *you'll soon recognize the need for a system* to structure all the progress your newfound levels of discipline, productivity and motivation engender.

In relation to other chapters, developing systems may seem like a dull, and perhaps even restrictive concern. To most people, especially creative types, the idea of using routines, statistics or any sort of predefined process is typically viewed as robotic, lifeless and dry. But while artists tend to resent monotony, strict order and direction, *the idea that a more systematic approach stifles creativity (rather than develops it) is distorted, imprisoning and flawed.*

To the contrary, with the methods we'll outline here you'll find that <u>systems actually enhance and cultivate creativity instead</u>, because the organization it provides frees up the attention and energy needed in order to do so.

In the same way that organizing your workspace facilitates a sense of order, organizing your *work process* will facilitate a sense of growth, and accelerate your sense of personal mastery. **Having a system lends frame to your artistic efforts no different than having a healthy skeletal structure lends frame to your physical body**, allowing a fluidity of movement the flesh, heart and nervous system - each analogous to the "organs" of motivation, willpower, productivity and intelligence - could never achieve by themselves.

Beyond the skeletal structure of humans and other vertebrates[1], remember that *all* living things have, at the very least, a DNA-pattern giving their cells the blueprint upon which to replicate by. That is, all living things, and *all things that are meant to function,* period - all:

- businesses

---

[1] Remember: all animal life without backbone or skeleton are called '*in*-vertebrates." This includes slugs, worms, jellyfish, sea anemones, octopus, squid, leeches, hag fish and cuttle fish, all of which are all boneless creatures. I hope I make my point clear.

- governmental boards

- public schools

- academic institutions

- medical establishments

- computer networks

- automobiles

- locomotives

- mass-transit systems

…and everything else that "works," works by the use of a system; in many cases a series of systems which layered on top of and complimenting one another.

This is a key philosophical point to grasp, because logically it follows that your own creative work should then entail the use of systems as well, however crude, simple or misguided such systems may initially be.

Unless you're working systematically, you're missing the forest for the trees - you could in fact be running on a treadmill incapable of even noticing it. Specifically, the benefits of a more systematic approach include (but are not limited to):

- increased confidence, because pursuing your goals in a more leveraged way eases feelings of anxiety and overwhelm

- faster improvements, because the use of systems is the best way to illustrate the cause-and-effect relationship shared between various events, or behaviors

- <u>enhanced teamwork</u>, because people tend to learn, focus and thrive most when they're in structured environments and

- <u>stronger willpower</u>, because not having to invent, concoct or push yourself through every task, problem or day leaves you with a larger threshold of energy in remainder.

Without the use of systems, creative work can tend to feel stressful, confusing and prone (or even destined) to failure. Likewise, *without* the use of systems, minor successes can seem circumstantial rather than inevitable consequences of fact, as they properly should.

Without systems, your creativity also runs the risk of becoming lackadaisical, random and prone (or even destined) to erosion and eventual loss. Unless you systematize your overall approach, you won't be streamlined enough to handle larger amounts of it either, or scientific enough to approach excellence in your chosen field.

Again, systems are, in effect, the skeletal structure to your "body of work": they lend frame to your creativity no different then a backbone or skeleton lends frame to your physical form.

But if systems are so vital, how exactly should one go about setting them up? Let's talk for a second about specific steps you can take to develop systems in ways that best complement your creative endeavors.

UNDERSTAND YOUR WORK AS A PROCESS

Understand the process your work calls for <u>before</u> you begin, because the process is what <u>defines</u> the work to begin with.

If you don't know the overall process, or underlying dynamic, a specific task is a component of, or a specific goal constituent to, *you'll waste your time, energy and money by misdirecting them on trivial tasks and activities,* and if you can't at least approximate what an overall procedure entails, *then you don't really know what you're doing.*

(In fact, in elementary physics, work is literally *defined* as "energy applied to accomplish a specific result" - not just simply "taking action" - a definition which implies having some semblance of a plan or a strategy devised beforehand.)

The tendency for most creative people however is to just start working and, in some cases, to spend their *entire lives* on only a series of small, minuscule projects while never finishing any large-scale, comprehensive one. Once most creative people are motivated to do something, if they can get themselves motivated at all, they tend to take up an attitude that says, " Well let's just do *something*," rather than calculate what's possible from a higher altitude.

Don't be that person, and if you are that person, *don't be that person anymore*. Always think about the steps and details a goal necessitates *first*, and always think about the specific end-result you want to accomplish *from the outset*, because that's what'll allow you to formulate more efficient, productive ways to get it done.

The irony here is that once you're systematic in how you approach things, <u>you actually become more productive by being lazy</u>. It's slightly counterintuitive, but once you grasp how something works systematically, or at least attempt to approach it that way, laziness becomes a productivity-enhancer, because <u>a little bit of laziness is what causes us to simplify and automate processes</u>.

As contrary to this book's theme as it may sound, **human laziness is a blessing**: it causes us to create routines, and routines allow us to use less energy while accomplishing the same, or even better, results. We'll cover this more in the next chapter, but here are a few examples…

For a blog-talk radio show I hosted in 2010, rather than develop *new* material for each episode, I simply read old articles live on air, and then held a question-and-answer session afterwards.

While *I started out* by developing new material for each show, after the first two I became overwhelmed, so when it came time to draft content for the third, I simply…

- organized the older blog posts, essays and newsletters I had sitting idly on my computer,

- categorized them into common subjects of interest ("how to get focused," "simple steps for reducing stress," "how to holistically build your health and energy," etc.),

- edited the articles to create a sense of seamlessness and clarity amongst what was originally various types of writing written at various times,

- found music to use during commercial breaks and intermissions

…and before long I had a thorough script for a two-hour-long self-help radio show that I was able to duplicate (both production and hosting) weekly, with relatively ease.

For my actual blog, Today's Transcendence, I duplicate most of the source code to speed up the formatting time for each entry.

Since I always start and end my blogs off in the same way, I simply *created a template-skeleton* of the basic HTML-code which always repeated, so whenever I start a new post I just copy and paste it into the editor. This cuts my editing time down to about *half.*[2]

Also on the blog, I use a lot of stock photography, not just because I like stock photography, but because the website I get the photos from has *a uniform set of dimensions* all their pictures adhere to. Originally, I'd get different images for a blog post from different online sources (Google, Flickr, Deviant-Art, etc.) and perform the time-wasting chore of resizing each of them to create a sense of consistency. Now however, once I found a dedicated site to get all of my pictures from, as they all have the same height, width and filetype extension, I no longer have to do any math or graphic design in order to compose a new post.

From these examples, you can see that:

- repurposing material

- creating "skeletons," or frameworks

- using repetition and uniformity and

- having templates for consistency

…are some of the principles that this system-based thinking is founded upon.

Another key principle for understanding your work as a process is to **know the overall aim your work is intended to serve**. Unlike attaining discipline, which is about mastery and refinement of a particular skill, developing systems, in contrast, is about strategizing your tasks

---

[2] I have a dread of monotonous labor. While everyone who knows me thinks of me as one of the most focused and disciplined people they've come across, the reality is that *I hate work*, and *that's* what motivates a lot of the organizational habits that I set up and influences the way I behave.

with a long-term objective in mind. Like Yin-and-Yang, you have to learn to balance both mindsets and sense when you're falling too far on either side of the dynamic. For instance:

- If you're an activist, think less about individual causes or the newfound social inequalities of the world, and *more about the long-term end result, or true change, you'd like your work to effect.* There are literally *millions* of problems out there that need to be addressed, but what's the specific problem that affects *you* or has meaning to you *personally?* How would a shift in focus towards *that* create a shift in your work on a day-to-day, structural level?

- If you're a musician, think less about specific tracks you'd like to record or specific bands you'd like to join or model yourself after, and *more about where you'd like to end up* and *how you'd like to position yourself* over time. What does music mean to you thematically? How will music, over the long-term, change (or integrate into) your life as a whole?

- If you're a blogger, think less about your posting schedule for the next month or specific pitfalls in your social-media marketing routine, and *more about the deeper purpose blogging serves for you, as well as the professional possibilities it can open up in the near future.* What would you like to become of your work down the line? What's the new phase of life your blog is transitioning you towards?

…because all of this will change your work in both a procedural and fundamental way.

But the real key to remember is that you have to understand, and approach, your work as a complete *process*, not simply a series of tasks. Don't waste time and energy expending it in ways that are a vague or undefined, nor in a manner that's minuscule or short-sighted. Always ask yourself the question, *"What am I doing? What's the overall process that this specific action is a part of, and what are the steps involved?"*

Later on in this chapter, I'll show you a special diagramming technique you can use to facilitate this type of systems-level thinking (as it'll help you to visualize the big picture), but first let's cover the second aspect of systems level-thinking, feedback and statistical measurement.

USE MEASUREMENT LIKE A MIRROR-REFLECTION

Just as systems serve as a skeletal structure for one's work, *measurement* - the quantification and assessment of said work, done objectively - serves as a mirror for one's progress, because **statistical measurement is the only accurate reflection of performance and efficiency.**

Just as a man needs a mirror when he goes to the barber, or a woman when she goes to her beautician, you also need a "mirror" of quantifiable feedback in order to honestly engage with your creative work, personal habits and even basic concerns, such as your financial behavior, as it's the only way to truly see what's happening for what it is.

This "reflection" of charts, data, measurements and numerical feedback is what'll provide you with both leverage and accountability: it'll help you notice the patterns and tendencies you otherwise wouldn't detect and it'll force you to address your ambitions in a mature, realistic way, no different than an actual mirror would bring to light the true nature of your appearance.

In fact it's been said that *the ability to chart data is one of the great inventions of contemporary civilization,* and although my historical knowledge isn't adequate enough to assess that claim technically, I agree with the sentiment in principle.

Remember, we human beings simply aren't *wired* to understand things objectively, mathematically, scientifically or purely as they are: like communication, literally everything we both experience gets *filtered* through the lens of our own personal biases, subconscious beliefs, emotional habits, petty little self-deceptions and more. This is to say that you and I are both virtually *incapable* of intuitively grasping:

- how effective our creative work actually is

- which aspects of our creative work are the most productive

- which aspects of our creative work are the *least,* or even

- how much creative work we actually complete to begin with.

So unless you install a feedback mechanism to tally and sort out your results, you won't have a guidepost to help you attune, refine or enhance what you're doing. **You can't refine an activity you don't systematically understand or statistically gauge** so, for instance…

To improve your spending habits, use a calendar (or make an Excel spreadsheet resembling a calendar) to account for all of your spending each day, using the daily amounts to then tally for each week and the weekly amounts for each month. You'll find *the simple thought of having to write an expenditure down* makes the needless ones less desirable and that truly seeing, objectively, exactly how much you spend on a specific item or trivial habit, over an extended period of time, puts things it perspective.

Likewise, to improve your eating habits, use a food-log to notate everything you eat, the times of day you eat at, how you feel both before *and* after the meal, and any other motivational ideas or insights which come to mind. This'll create, again, a sense of accountability by providing you with an accurate sense of where some of your biggest opportunities and most dangerous pitfalls are, which are both usually counter-intuitive and nearly invisible.

Even something as simple as a daily schedule - a journal that archives what you *should do* versus what *end up* doing do for each hour of the day - will provide you with <u>huge</u> insight into your habitual routines, your most motivating behaviors and your most destructive idiosyncrasies.

I still use a financial calendar to this day: because I can see (again, objectively) a sharp contrast between how I spend when money's running versus whenever it's slow. <u>Now I have a practical, personalized guide for how to cut back even when times are good</u>, so that I can hold on to the good times for that much longer.

Similarly, the daily schedule gave me stronger self-awareness as well. Using it back in college, I noticed that

- my creativity and attention-span was strongest during certain time-windows of day, and that

- my emotional state was affected by the type of space I was in

Generally speaking, I found that I thrive and feel rejuvenated in small intimate groups and open, outdoor settings, but feel confined and inhibited whenever in overcrowded, indoor ones.

The schedule showed me that I'd feel drained by going to a packed Greek Fraternity probate and exhausted when at a congested house-party for instance, but replenished when in an apartment just talking with two or three other friends or simply walking the campus grounds of a neighboring university. It seems obvious in hindsight, since I'm an introvert, but the measurement is what originally exposed this to me.[3]

---

[3] For more on introversion - on the strengths of having such a personality style, and methods for creating a way of life that honors it (rather than condemns) - see <u>Quiet: The Power of Introverts in a World That Can't Stop Talking</u> by Susan Cain

This technique really takes off when you start applying it to your creative skills. When blogging, I measure how many people like and comment on each specific post, so I know which subjects are the most engaging. When writing, I measure how many words and how much time I spend actually producing words on each specific day, so I can set my writing goals to push myself more realistically. You can do an infinite number of similar tactics if you take the time to truly think of it.

As a note, when you start measuring yourself and forget to gather data one day, for any reason, which is inevitable, start annotating right from where you currently are, not from where you left off. If you forget to note things down one day - if you get too busy, too lazy or anything of the sort - do not try to catch up and "remember" missed entries, because you'll fall into a habit of forgetting and recalling rather than actually measuring. Whatever stats you miss out on, whether it be for a day, for a week or even for an entire year, consider it a loss and start measuring again from where you are.[4]

But again, **statistical measurement is the mirror of performance and efficiency.** Use charts, grids, tally sheets and dashboards to provide yourself with quantifiable feedback to grow off of and you'll be surprised at some of the insights you'll gain.

- For spending, use a calendar to get a visual display of how you spend, on what, and tally that for the day, for the week and for the month.

- If you're writing, calculate how many words, lines, paragraphs and sections you draft in an hour's or a day's work, and how much time you spend in dedicated, focused, undisturbed writing time for each session.

- If you blog, track how many likes or hits each blog post receives, what times of day to best publish new material, and anything else your analytics allow you to.

- In general, track how you choose to spend your free time and how those choices affect your state of mind, or what you eat, as well as how much you eat, and how that affects your overall attitude.

---

[4] Like with anything, never be too hard on yourself if you slip up. The idea here is to get some feedback on your behavior in real-time, not caught up in the drudgery of forcing yourself to quantify every single activity. Never hold guilt about any mistakes you make because you will make them, eventually, no matter how meticulous you try to be. Conquering yourself is a practical and mechanical activity first, not a reason to internalize shame or anything of the sort.

(Note: *DO NOT attempt to tally and measure several concerns at the same time*: you'll get so inundated with the quantification of your every move that none of it'll do you any good. Choose one of the fields mentioned above, for example, or any other concern of importance to you, and hone in on that for at least *a month* before switching or phasing over to anything else. I suggest starting with the financial calendar, at least as a test, as this'll give you an *immediate* feel for what I mean when I speak of the leverage, accountability and realizations that come with numerical feedback.)

It's ironic: a lot of people want to be more productive, eat healthier or otherwise become more disciplined in life, but the idea of statistically gauging their progress never occurs to them. I'm not saying to condemn anyone, only to point out, again, that *we're not instinctively wired to do things like quantify, measure or chart our behavior or results*…it doesn't naturally come to us as the sensible thing to do.

Remember, we humans are really *animals* first who respond and react on the basis of animalistic stimuli; something as helpful and self-evident as tracking or logistically measuring our interests won't occur to us on the basis of interest alone.

REFERENCES AND FURTHER CONCERNS…

For more on the value and use of statistics, charts, graphs and so on, see <u>The Visual Display of Quantitative Information</u> by Edward R. Tufte.

But again, the idea here is simple: you can't refine or enhance an activity or dynamic you don't statistically gauge or understand, which is why you have to become somewhat of a scientist in regards to your creative goals.

As a means of helping you to think more systematically, *try creating "mind-maps"*: graphical *information-webs that allow you to generate ideas, structure plans and correlate knowledge in free-form.*

Say, for example, you wanted to generate an outline for a book of your own, or perhaps take notes on this specific chapter, try creating a multi-layered brainstorm that looks something like this (see next two pages):

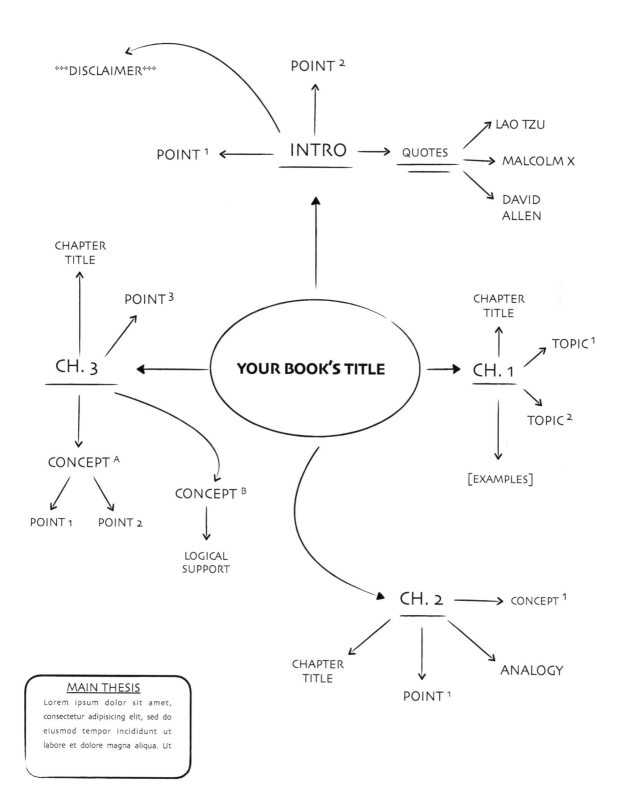

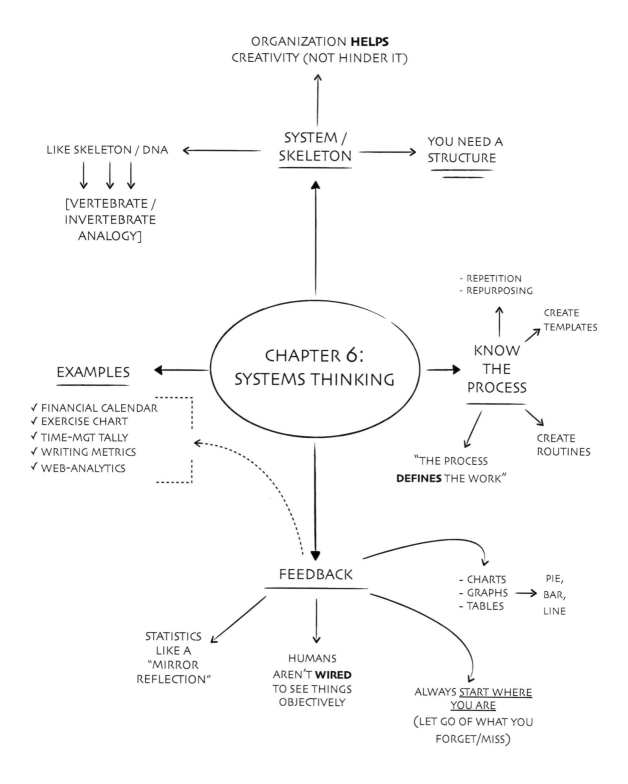

ORGANIZATION **HELPS**
CREATIVITY (NOT HINDER IT)

SYSTEM /
SKELETON

LIKE SKELETON / DNA

[VERTEBRATE /
INVERTEBRATE
ANALOGY]

YOU NEED A
STRUCTURE

- REPETITION
- REPURPOSING

CREATE
TEMPLATES

CHAPTER 6:
SYSTEMS THINKING

KNOW
THE
PROCESS

EXAMPLES

✓ FINANCIAL CALENDAR
✓ EXERCISE CHART
✓ TIME-MGT TALLY
✓ WRITING METRICS
✓ WEB-ANALYTICS

CREATE
ROUTINES

"THE PROCESS
DEFINES THE WORK"

FEEDBACK

- CHARTS
- GRAPHS
- TABLES

PIE,
BAR,
LINE

STATISTICS
LIKE A
"MIRROR
REFLECTION"

HUMANS
AREN'T **WIRED**
TO SEE THINGS
OBJECTIVELY

ALWAYS START WHERE
YOU ARE
(LET GO OF WHAT YOU
FORGET/MISS)

The process is simple: rather than write the title at the *top* of the page, write it in the center, and then create nodes for each subtopic which branch out from there:

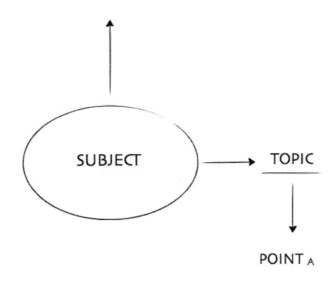

In time, you'll eventually have several subtopics or concerns each branching out into further subdivisions themselves, like so:

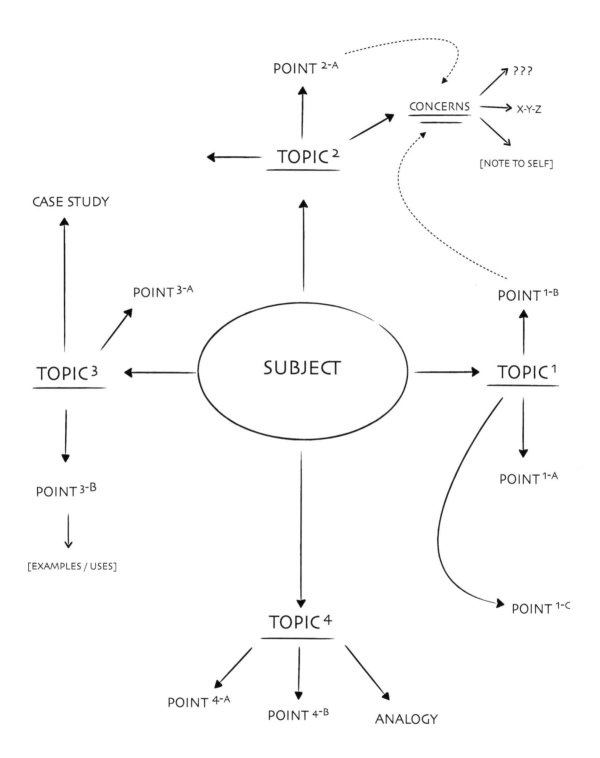

What makes mind-mapping so effective is that _they replicate actual, real-time thinking_. While normal note taking techniques are linear - they suppose that you're thinking sequentially, as in "First I'm going to do this, then I'm going to do that," - mind-maps are more holistic: they know that your thoughts tend to offshoot and divert into other thoughts, so they have you "map" a visual representation of that process. They let you form ideas freely while still having a written structure to capture everything that occurs.It's a mind "map" in the sense that it helps you to navigate the geography of your own artistic intelligence, which is, of course, more prone to a random, sporadic intensity than a predictable, traceable expression. [1]

The best part is that _it's easy_ and that **there's literally no limit to how they can be applied.** I personally use mind-maps to plan out everything: blogposts, lectures, my book and research notes to what I'm going to do for the day, an argument I want to present, trips out of town and so on. It's now become part of the fundamental way I write.

You can also design mind-maps in a tree-diagram fashion, thereby creating a fusion between the free-form nature of the map and a more sequential methodology in one layout, like so:

---

[1] There are some websites and computer software (such as bubbl.us) to help digitize the process, but my suggestion, especially if you're just starting is to keep it handwritten and natural.

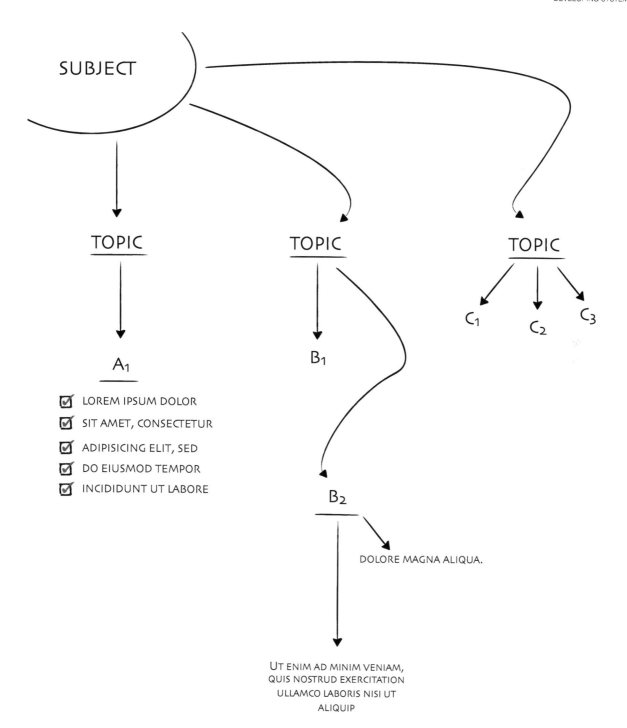

SUBJECT

TOPIC

TOPIC

TOPIC

A_1

☑ LOREM IPSUM DOLOR
☑ SIT AMET, CONSECTETUR
☑ ADIPISICING ELIT, SED
☑ DO EIUSMOD TEMPOR
☑ INCIDIDUNT UT LABORE

B_1

C_1 C_2 C_3

B_2

DOLORE MAGNA ALIQUA.

UT ENIM AD MINIM VENIAM,
QUIS NOSTRUD EXERCITATION
ULLAMCO LABORIS NISI UT
ALIQUIP

Remember, mind-mapping is simply a more accurate, visual representation of how the human thought-process, especially a creative thought process, tends to exhibit itself.

When you think, you don't think right to left or strictly up and down in a linear fashion, as we're taught to write. If you're being creative, once you have an idea, you then have another, but then a third, fourth or fifth that best relates to the first rather than the second, as they continue to bounce off of one another in nonlinear, unpredictable ways.

I'm suggesting you use mind-maps to plan your work because this'll help you not only to be more systematic, but to domesticate, tame and rein in your more powerful ideas, so you can enjoy the depths of your creative zone for a lengthened, sustained duration of time.

I'm also suggesting you use mind maps to plan your work *before* you start, as this'll help you to see it on a grand enough scale to start automating the process. But the reality is *you can use mind maps for anything*: articles you want to write, books you have to take notes on, a day of activities you need to structure (where the subject becomes the day, the topics become calls to make, writing goals, work-related tasks and additional errands) or even an important discussion you're going to have (where the topics then become, of course, subcomponents of your argument). Again, there's literally no limit to how they can be applied.

Use the examples above to try a few for yourself, take a break to reflect, and let's continue…

CH. 7: HOW TO CULTIVATE WILLPOWER

"WILLPOWER IS AN ENERGETIC RESPONSE FOUND IN THE BODY
AND MIND, NOT A VIRTUE TO BE FOUND IN ONE'S CHARACTER."

"Habit took the advantage of inattention; inclination
was sometimes too strong for reason."
~ Benjamin Franklin

"It is foolish to presume our power of resolve is constant."
~ Troilus (in Shakespeare's "Troilus & Cressida")

THE ORIGINS OF "WILLPOWER"

Just as our notion of time-management originates from the industrial revolution, **our notion of willpower originates from the industrial *age*.** The way we think about willpower - the way we approach cultivating more of it - originates from a *cultural* transformation which parallels the industrial one, as they happened during the same time period and share some of the same causative factors.

This period, known as the Victorian Age, or Victorian Era, is best known not just for the preeminence of classical English culture and fashion, but also (as mentioned in Chapter 5, and more importantly for our purposes here) for the transition <u>away from</u> small, communal villages and <u>into</u> large, industrial cities, because *alongside this socio-demographic transition, there was also a more "ethical" transition as well: a transition of values <u>away from</u> traditional, religious, Christian beliefs and <u>towards</u> a belief in independence and self-reliance.*

So as people began to:

- live in cities rather than on farms

- work in factories rather than on land

- ride trains rather than horses

- use clocks and calendars to allocate work rather than environmental cues

- think about productivity in more mechanical form (developing terms like "time-management")

…and value urban life over its rural equivalent, <u>they also began to think about themselves *as individuals*, rather than as part of a collective whole.</u>

The new, busy populous city life of the industrial revolution wasn't just about trains, clocks and manufacturing, but also about personal freedom and the redefinition of human life, because, on both sides of the Atlantic, <u>people were no longer confined to the small locality and social norms of an isolated, agrarian village</u>. Whereas in rural times, for instance, your social network consisted of no more than a hundred people, all of whom knew you since the day you were born, went to the same school as you, attended the same church and so on, in industrialized times, *your social network was potentially limitless*: you could now meet anyone, be anyone, leave your past behind you, neglect your upbringing and do just about anything while still retaining a degree of anonymity.

The Church worried about this, of course. Religious institutions, accustomed to the power and authority they held over tight-knit, communal towns, worried that these new social liberties would bring about new forms of spiritual decay; that the mechanical progress of the industrial revolution, with its more progressive implications for human life, would lead people to "fall into temptation" and bring about a "rampant moral depravity" from which society would never recover.

So as Americans began to question and challenge the traditional, Victorian notions of ethical conduct and religious obedience (they were now free from the social pressures which chained them to it), the Church was forced to find a new way to reach out to the American public.

"Willpower" was thus the Church's reactionary campaign: it became a key slogan in their quest to retain influence over a morphing society with a transitory sense of ethical code. So in came an influx of literature such as Samuel Smiles *Self-Help* in 1859, Frank Channing Haddock's *The Power of Will* in 1907 and so on, all sharing the same idea: that one could live a somewhat of a religious life - that one could withstand the enticements of the industrialized world even without the normal structure and limitations of a deeply-religious, communal village - simply by honoring the call to morality that lie inside him. The idea was that even without regular church attendance, or any religious inclination whatsoever, God places within us not only an internal moral compass, but the force and resolve to follow it successfully at all times; the process of acknowledging this compass and obeying this force, was "having willpower."

In the recent book <u>Willpower: Rediscovering the Greatest Human Strength</u>, a contemporary read we'll explore later, co-author John Tierney says:

> "As farmers moved into industrial cities during the nineteenth century, they were no longer constrained by village churches, social pressures and universal beliefs. The Protestant Reformation had made religion more individualistic, and the Enlightenment weakened faith in any kind of dogma whatsoever. Victorians thus saw themselves as living in a time of transition as the moral certainties and rigid institutions of medieval

Europe died away. A popular topic of debate was whether morality could even *survive* without religion (emphasis mine).

Many Victorians came to doubt religious principles on theoretical grounds, but they kept pretending to be faithful believers because they considered it their public duty to preserve morality. Today it's easy to mock their hypocrisy and prudery, but considering all of the new temptations available to them, it was hardly neurotic to be searching for new sources of strength. As Victorians fretted over moral decay and the social pathologies concentrated in cities, they also looked for something more tangible than divine grace, some internal strength that could protect even an atheist.

They began using the term *willpower* because of the folk notion that some kind of force was involved - some inner equivalent to the steam which was powering the Industrial Revolution itself…"

So keep this in mind: Victorians truly believed that the industrial revolution would bring an end to Christian life, and **our very notion of willpower and what it means stems from the literature and propaganda created in light of that fear**.

It's only recently actually, with the work of researchers like Dr. Roy Baumeister, Walter Mischel and others, that we've come to see willpower through a scientific lens, free from the range of any religious aim or residual tone.

This contemporary, scientific notion views willpower simply as an energy-dynamic in one's body and mind; as an energy source we need to find ways to preserve, recover and increase in order to make better decisions, including those that require us to "willpower," as in force, ourselves through a challenge in the traditional sense.

We'll discuss this more in the next section, but here, I just want you to take heed that your notions of willpower, even if you don't use Christian terminology, may be, in essence, religious rather than scientific. I'm asking you to cultivate willpower by first letting go of it as a spiritual ideal, because until you do, it'll only be a vague concept that tends to inspire guilt (as you'll always eventually fail to be "delivered from temptation"), rather than practical, objective advice you can take action and build strategies upon.

Ask yourself the question, "Do I think about willpower as a moral obligation, almost like some sacred virtue I'm incomplete and sinful for not observing, or do I think about willpower in a more mature, grounded and technical way?"

Again, you can't cultivate willpower until you demystify the process: until you stop thinking about it in relation to your soul or identity and, instead, more in relation to your physiology and energetic state; as an energetic response that has both physical and psychic, or mental, aspects to it; until you get more in tune with the conditions that govern the peaks and valleys of these dynamics.

WILLPOWER IS A SOURCE OF ENERGY, NOT A VIRTUE

So although, as discussed in Chapter 1, willpower builds itself indirectly, there *is* a small composite, or type, of willpower that works in this traditional, direct way, but it's based on a subtle source of energy, not physical force. Again, you cultivate willpower by freeing yourself of the old-school, Victorian delusion of it as a spiritual virtue, and by replacing that with a stronger, internal gauge of your personal, physiological system.

You can think of it as mental athleticism or mental endurance: it includes more obvious concerns such as *making sure to get sleep* and *eating sensibly* (both of which become far less obvious as you become more active), but also the not-so-intuitive techniques of…

  - taking frequent breaks

  - making decisions early in the day

  - working in fragments rather than wholes and

  - developing routines that preserve your mental energy rather than squander it.

The next section, *Willpower Applications*, will cover these specific methods and more, but for now, I want you to grasp the point, to truly see for yourself, that when we talk about cultivating willpower, what we're talking about is cultivating energy and *avoiding fatigue* of both the physical and psychic sort. It's about getting a better sense of when your mind and body are off, doing things to prevent that from happening in the first place and doing even more to amplify it whenever it's on.

Technically speaking, **willpower is recovered by either rest or glucose** (the sugar in foods, preferably foods that rate low on something called the "glycemic index"), **but depleted by making decisions**, because any time you have to decide, deliberate, consider, weigh options or analyze at all, your brain's utilizing glucose for that activity; fatigue is then simply a signal that you're low on such glucose-based power.

A good analogy is to think of your willpower as a battery: you're ability to "will" yourself to write a new story, design an original graphic, or mix a series of tracks in ProTools can be easily squandered by the other "applications" of life you have running in the background, no different then a smartphone or tablet PC. Just as a device charges best when it's completely *off*, and preserves battery when it's not constantly used, so you too must design a strategy that keeps your energy high throughout the day, so as to reserve some charge for your artistic endeavors.[1]

This is especially important because creative work is all *mental*. You have to guard, secure and attend to your psychic energy gauge because it's what drives your creative productivity in the first place.

Here's some specific examples…

WILLPOWER APPLICATIONS

1. Take Frequent Breaks: This first issue, to break frequently and intermittently, rather than only once or twice after long intervals of labor, is crucial because *your willpower - no different than your time, money or attention - is limited and confined for each 24-hour period.*

If you think about it, our concept of breaks and recess, like our concept of willpower, also originates from historic, industrialized times, where labor was primarily physical and monotonous, not creative or knowledge-oriented. In today's world however, you'll achieve more by taking frequent breaks than you ever will by working obsessively, and "you stay fully engaged by taking up the mentality of a sprinter, not a marathon runner."[2]

---

[1] The term psychologist Roy Baumeister uses is "Ego-Depletion." Any task or activity that trains one's psychic energy - writing, arguing, shopping when on a budget, or even having a phone conversation - depletes the willpower storage we're talking about here. Baumeister also sees "Self-regulation failure as the major social pathology of our time."

[2] Tony Schwartz in his book, The Power of Full Engagement.

Everything in nature operates by cycles, including your mental and physical energy, so just at you need to rest at night in order to sleep, you also need to rest intermittently during the day, especially during a creative or intellectual assignment, in order to stay focused.

Whereas the human sleep cycle is governed by something called the "circadian rhythm," which you're probably familiar with, the day-energy cycle is governed by something called the *UL-tradian rhythm*, which graphs like so:

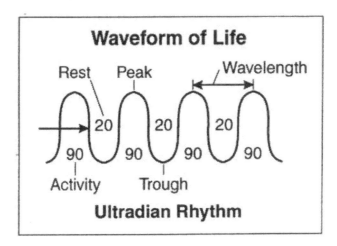

It's a fascinating concept to research if you're interested, but the general idea is that you want to *take a break and completely detach from what you're doing every 90 to 120 minutes*.

There was a more specific version of this I used last year where I'd:

- work for fifty minutes

- break for ten

- work for another fifty

- break for ten

…and *then completely detach for thirty*, but I find the every ninety or two-hour version simpler and easier to maintain.

Again, take frequent breaks and *avoid exhaustion*, because if you tire yourself incessantly, you'll make poor decisions, lose creative ideas, communicate deficiently and miss out on opportunities you're simply too drained to even realize. <u>Don't treat your mind like a field-slave</u>; realize that <u>creative work exists in a psychic realm</u>, not a material one, so when you lose the ability to concentrate, that's your body's feedback as to its natural needs.

If you stay in "work mode" and pass your energy-threshold just to finish one more paragraph, process one more client or edit one more audio track, you'll pay *for* it with a lack of focus, poor memory, decreased creativity and bad sleep at night, let alone all the mistakes you'll inevitably make during that session. Listen to your body and take frequent breaks to replenish yourself *every ninety minutes*.

2. Create Routines: Similarly, as discussed in the chapter on systems, use routines to conserve willpower, because the more routinized and systematic your work-process becomes, the less decision-making and conscious thought you'll have to expend while performing it.

For instance, if I sit down at my desk to write a chapter, once I'm motivated to start writing, I have to *think about* and *decide* what chapter and section I'm going to write.

If I have the day off, and I know there's a series of errands that I have to accomplish that specific day, but only a vague notion of what those errands are, I have to *think about* and *decide* the order in which to perform them, which ones to postpone or neglect, and whether or not I should write before, after or during that performance.

If I have a series of writing-related correspondence to make - if I have to email my printer, call my assistant and ask to borrow office-space from a friend - but haven't predefined those obligations beforehand, I have to *think about* and *decide* the best time to call or ask them, and concoct a rough draft of how I should go about that negotiation.

If however, I create an outline with miniature schedules and deadlines for each section, establish a specific range of writing time for each day (preferably early in the morning, before most people wake up), use a mind-map to categorize my errands for the weekend *as they arise* and create a folder with rough drafts for all significant correspondence (as well as establish several time-windows for possible correspondence), then when I sit down to write my chapter, I know everything's lined up, and this is important because <u>it's the only guarantee I have that my storage of willpower will go specifically to creative work</u> rather than merely peripheral concerns.

It's almost like budgeting, but you're budgeting energy as opposed cash; psychic attention, creativity and decision-making power as opposed to saving accounts or a weekly check. You need to routinize and systematize your work so you don't squander willpower into micro-managing the details; so you don't spend your free time and free energy *reacting* and *firefighting* to problems rather than constructing and building solutions.

Become a bit more "obsessive-compulsive" about your work-structure, and your future as a creative professional as a whole, if you want to begin conquering larger stocks of it, because, as discussed in Chapter 3, *the creative goals you need willpower for aren't like the jobs you've been paid for*, not only because creative work, by itself, *does not* entitle you to compensation, but also because <u>creative work, from the outset, isn't predefined</u>. If you don't define and systematize it yourself beforehand, you'll deplete most of your energy (willpower) simply ascertaining what it entails as you go along instead of actually working…

Again, create routines to automate and predefine your work as much as you can, because the more routinized and systematic your artistic work is, the less decision-making, conscious thought and willpower you'll expend simply getting ready to perform it.

3. Watch Your Diet: Also crucial to sustaining willpower is your diet. Specifically, make sure to eat foods that are *low* on the glycemic index rather than high.

The glycemic index is a measurement of how quickly the human body absorbs the sugar-content of particular foods. Generally speaking, *high*-glycemic foods release their sugar rapidly, providing high spikes of energy that consequent in drastic lows, but *low*-glycemic foods release their sugar gradually, providing a sustained sense of energy that keeps one's willpower steady and manageable.

<u>High glycemic foods *to avoid* (when in need of willpower) include</u>: carbohydrates like white bread, pasta, rice, low-fiber cereals, potatoes, instant potatoes and anything baked or sweetened.

<u>Low glycemic foods *to have* (when in need of willpower) include</u>: fruits and fruit juice, like oranges, pineapple, apples, kiwis, grapes, mangoes peas and beans, carrots, nuts, seeds, high-fiber, bran cereal and so on.

Simply eat for energy, not taste, during times when you need to be energized - reserve your general eating preferences for more negligible time-slots - and you'll be fine.

4. Fragment the Work: Also, in tandem with the analogy of working in sprints, not marathons, *always segment your work into fractions*; into small fragments you can easily conceive of grasping your energy around.

For instance, this book is fragmented into chapters, which were then fragmented further into subsections that are *far* easier to willpower myself through writing than an entire book. In fact, much of the content here originally began as earlier blog work I've done that, as a daily exercise, gradually phased me into the writing practice which laid the foundation for this text as a whole.

If you have trouble conquering a specific challenge in life, <u>fragment that challenge into subcomponents</u>, rather than see it as an integrated whole and you'll have a better, more realistic starting point from which to improve.

For example, in a blog post about dating, I once encouraged men to build their dating skills one step at time, to:

"Learn to look at the whole courting process as a sequence of events, and *just focus on successfully transitioning from one phase to the next.*

This was a big one for me, because not only did I learn to focus on improving one area of my 'game' a time, <u>I also became indifferent to the overall outcome</u>. (Women can sense when you're interested but at the same time dis-attached, and it's *very* attractive…it shows that you have a sense of self-control.)

But most guys don't get this step-by-step approach: as soon as they realize a woman's interested in them, they skip the natural stages, try to take things too far, too soon and somehow expect something to happen. This is a turn-off for women, *because you're not building any anticipation in her mind.*

So a more sequence-oriented approach is good for several reasons:

5. You get to improve your skills by focusing on each aspect separately

6. She feels more comfortable around you and

7. You separate yourself from almost *all* of the other guys she's dealt with (which is key).

Also, since you're the man, know that *it's always on you to take things to the next level* - know that you're the one who's going to have to take the risk and progress at each step of the game. Deal with it…

Again, everything's easier if you just take the "one-step-at-a-time" mentality:

- If you're not the best at approaching women and starting conversations, just focus on that until you feel comfortable with it.

- If you're not the best at getting phone numbers or email, just focus on that until it feels natural.

- If you're not the best at setting up dates with a woman and getting her to follow through, just focus on that, so on and so forth.

It's really just like learning anything else…"

I didn't see it at the time, but I was really suggesting that one learns best through a fragmented, isolationistic, philosophy rather than the more highly promoted, "holistic" one.

Until you break a task, goal, project, ambition or even a basic problem down to its essential components, won't even be able to even conceptualize accomplishing it in any tangible form. Remember to fragment your creative work into blocks you can actually tackle (preferably within the time-span of a few, frequent breaks).

The best part about the fragmenting approach is that it allows you to distinguish exactly *where* your problems are, so that you can technically diagnose what may currently seem like a complex, overbearing predicament or responsibility.

5. Experiment; Don't Commit: Lastly, take up the mentality of scientist who *experiments* and *tests* things out rather than commits to them up front.

Psychologically speaking, it's a lot easier to remain committed, focused, disciplined and willed towards something you see as an experiment rather than something you see yourself as tied to contractually. It's counter-intuitive, but in the same way you wouldn't *get married* at the start of your dating life, you shouldn't "marry" a particular long-term goal or creative project until you've had enough experience to maturely identify its probability for success.

<u>Be a scientist who does everything as a test</u>. Do things in small fragments, to see what kind of results you get *first*, and once you find out what works, gradually scale upwards.

Stop thinking you need to start off with a great, skyrocketing idea that's going to have major impact or requires a significant financial investment, and start experimenting until you find:

- what complements your personality and particular strengths

- what gets you the results that you want

- what you enjoy doing and

- what you can see yourself being dedicated to "for a minute."

Big goals, especially when they're ideas you're unsure of, create pressure, which, as discussed in Chapter 2, is where most procrastination comes from. In the worst case scenario, if you can't forecast whether or not it's even going to work, you might end up just speculating: wasting time, energy and money on the front end to find that it was a bad idea only after you lose out.

This is where a lot of otherwise extremely promising individuals fall short: they have a great idea about something unrealistically grandiose and promising *before they even begin*, because in their hyper-creative head, it seems like a perfect plan.

For instance, a few years ago I started a writing club (as I was first starting the book and wanted to mastermind with a few others) and told a poet friend of mine about the idea.

"Yeah, that's a great idea." he said. *"We can get you a set up at XYZ venue, because my friend does promotion over there. We can even get it popping on campus and start a poetry <u>movement</u>!"*

I said, "*Yeah…you know that sounds good, but <u>let's just see how the first meeting goes</u>, and then take it from there.*"

I said that only because I was being realistic: it's much easier to be disciplined, focused and willed around a single meeting, then it is around an entire poetry "movement" (whatever that is). It's simply too vague and *one should never be carried away by the enthusiasm of a new idea simply because it sounds promising.*

Of course, you may be thinking, "…but I don't want to do small things, I want to do *big* things. I want to have an impact eventually." and you should. The tendency however is that when you strike gold - when you find an opportunity that works - you'll find it has momentum on it's own; you'll have an intuitive sense of it finding you, rather than the opposite.

So don't be like my poetic friend. Don't speculate or get eager unnecessarily. Test the waters first and be a scientist who experiments with his hypotheses before he proclaims them.

Remember that <u>a lot of conquering yourself is simply accepting reality for what it is</u>; acknowledging the actual feedback existence furnishes to you, not simply your personal ideals about how it should work. Here, I'm not saying don't be dedicated to your overall goals, but that when it comes to particular methods and specific projects, always start small, experiment and scale up based on feedback first. Never overextend yourself based on pure dreams and conjecture, because you may start something and realize it's not for you.

<u>And remember that you're constantly learning</u>, which implies that the vast majority of ideas you have *aren't* going to work. When it comes to specific goals, you can't be attached to a single method of getting it done. Be resolute in purpose, but formless in strategy, and willpower will become more realistic, less superhuman, attainment.

But experimenting, breaking frequently, eating for energy, creating routines and fragmenting your creative work are all merely examples. Take some time to truly think about willpower as an energy dynamic and you'll soon realize dozens of personalized strategies you can devise to cultivate it in your own way.

REFERENCES AND FURTHER CONCERNS...

Again, **willpower is an energetic-response found in the body and mind, not a religious virtue to be found in one's character**. Let go of the industrial-age, Victorian notion of willpower as that which you can rely on to "fight the devil" or resist temptation, and instead, **cultivate a stronger, systematic internal gauge of the behavioral factors governing your physical and mental energy** so as to save, garner and replenish your creativity and decision-making strength for tasks where it's significantly needed.

> "We have no way of knowing how much our ancestors exercised self-control in earlier days, but it seems likely that they were under less strain. During the Middle Ages for instance, most people were peasants who put in long, dull days in fields, frequently accompanied by prodigious amounts of ale. They weren't angling for promotions at work or trying to climb the social ladder, so there wasn't a premium on diligence, or a great need for sobriety). Their villages didn't offer many obvious temptations beyond alcohol, sex or plain old sloth. *Virtue was generally enforced by a desire to avoid public disgrace rather than by any zeal to achieve human perfection.*"

For more on this contemporary framework of willpower - one based on scientific research rather than ecclesiastical fear - see either <u>Willpower: Rediscovering the Greatest Human Strength</u>, co-written by Roy Baumeister and John Tierney (quoted above) or <u>The Willpower Instinct: How Self-Control Works, Why It Matters & How You Can Get More Of It</u> by Kelly McGonigal.[3]

Also, <u>The Power of Full-Engagement: Managing Energy, Not Time, Is the Key to High Performance & Personal Renewal</u>, by Jim Loehr and Tony Schwartz, provides a good, action-oriented layout for developing willpower, though, ironically, they never used the term itself in description of their approach.

---

[3] The saying, "Willpower is an energetic response in the body and mind, not a religious virtue" comes from McGonigal, but Baumeister's work is what provided the historic context.

CONCLUSION

"THE QUEST FOR PRODUCTIVITY IS AN
INDIRECT PATH TO A STRONGER IDENTITY."

*"The next level, by definition, is something you
can't see and you can't understand."*
~ Eben Pagan

"Adversity introduces a man to himself."
~ anonymous

CONCLUSION...

In conclusion, remember that <u>willpower is an indirect game</u>: that you can only conquer yourself through ways that are subtle and counter-intuitive, not obvious or straightforward, and that the skills each chapter was dedicated to can only be reverse-engineered into existence. For example, you...

Overcome procrastination *indirectly* through self-esteem,

Attain discipline *indirectly* through a desire for mastery,

Raise productivity *indirectly* through focus and concentration,

Build motivation *indirectly* through a sense of empowerment,

Cultivate willpower *indirectly* through proper energy-governance, and

...lastly, all of these factors are enhanced and refined *indirectly* through a systematic approach to the results they culminate in. Remember this, and never force or compel yourself towards these aims, as that would ignore the subtle dynamics involved and may undermine the entire effort to begin with.

Also remember that <u>there's a subtle conspiracy against self-discipline</u>: that in our entertainment-driven, technologically-inundated, hyper-consumerist society, conquering yourself requires you to develop a unique mindset and an independent culture that shelters and shields the discipline you've attained from these influences, often by running diametrically opposed to them.

HIGHER PRODUCTIVITY LEADS TO A STRONGER IDENTITY

"Self-regulation *failure* is the major social pathology of our time;" the major mental dysfunction plaguing our society today.[1] That is, the *lack* of self-control - the root issue this book was written to address - isn't just an individual problem nor simply a rare skill to obtain…*its absence has now become tantamount to a preeminent psychological disease.*

As our entire world suffers from attention deficit, and as there's endless opportunities for distraction, temptation and indulgence in today's world, we're being pushed out of our ability to focus without even realizing it, and this is tragic **because a mind without the ability to focus is, in essence, a man without the ability to act towards any purposeful end**.

So as a final thought, consider that just as the Industrial Age brought us a new language for productivity ("time-management") and a new conceptual framework for inner-strength, ("willpower"), we're now going through an Information Age which, with its transition from mechanization to digitization; *from an economy based on the technical mastery of manufacturing processes to an one based on the creative mastery of data and knowledge*, likewise necessitates a similar process of redefinition and change: both a new language for work and a new conceptual framework for the human identity.

We're at the dawn of another century and at the onset of the next millennium, shifting into an entirely different habitat, but don't get it confused: this transition is simply another chapter in the tale of our collective saga; the next "act" in the divine theatre, or on the dramatic stage, of civilization itself. While the actors are different and the setting has evolved, but the basic theme and premise - the constant reinterpretation of mortal existence - is the same.

This theme and premise is, in actuality, a subtle dynamic which, since our lives tend to center around our own personal dramas, happens too gradually to notice through instinct alone. I'm mentioning the social perspective here because I want you to **understand this book within that trajectory of change**. Consider the implications of what this book has taught you not simply in relation to your own challenges and goals, *but as the beginning to a new syntax we'll need to remain self-directed in a hyper-digitized world.*

The next "city" we're all moving to is cyberspace itself. As time moves forward, the reality we'll come to occupy and inhabit will itself come to be more of an abstraction - more of a world ruled by the boundless nature of conceptual ideas rather than the parameters of tangible form. This abstract environment, particularly due to its commercialized leanings, requires a new type of

---

[1] This is another quote originally from Dr. Roy Baumeister.

thinking in order to retain discipline and self-control while dwelling within the confines of it, lest one fall victim to the pathologies and dysfunctions now becoming cultural norms...

Further, in the same way that technological progress always brings about redefinition - just as the shift from an agrarian society to an industrial one, as well as the current shift from an industrial society to a digital one, have both brought about slightly more independent, scientific notions of human nature, ethical behavior, power, energy and so on - you too, in relation to your own progress, will likewise have to redefine yourself and grow comfortable with the "revolution" and "new age" of creative power this book is meant to engender within you.

That is, to conquer yourself is to go through a series of "technological advancements" and "scientific discoveries" in respect to your own life, on the internal frontier of your own psyche, but "the next level, by definition, is something you can't see and you can't understand," so don't be like the Victorian Church and <u>don't be a Luddite in reference to your creative growth</u>.[2]

Don't fear the shifts in identity, behavior or even in moral code your progress will implicitly ask of you, because that calling comes from a place you don't yet have the perspective to question and because **the quest for higher productivity, on both a personal and social level, is an indirect path towards a stronger identity.**

Remember: many of the dystopian, cataclysmic fears we've held about the future - the panics Science Fiction writers prey upon, for example - *have never come to pass.* We humans tend to associate progress, change and the acquisition of power with tragedy, disaster and grief, but just as we've historically overblown the consequences of adapting steam power, electricity and many other technologies we wouldn't dare live without now, most of the consequences you may envision for your own future (adapting to what your goals mean for future versions of yourself) are similarly overblown, drawn out of proportion and governed by fear.

---

[2] The Luddites were a group of English workers who destroyed the machinery in cotton mills and wood factories, as they believed these workshops threatened their jobs. *Neo-Luddism*, in turn, is "a movement of passive resistance to the increasingly bizarre and frightening technologies of the Computer Age." Jerry Mander's book, <u>Four Arguments for the Elimination of Television</u>, for instance, could be seen as having a Neo-Luddite philosophical bent.

If you have any reservations about what success will bring to you, <u>check your premises</u>. Don't let anxiety undermine your ambition, because you can't be motivated to act in a world you believe is doomed to misfortune, or towards a goal you worry may signal doom and misfortune for you.[3]

Progress in the human psyche - new levels of accomplishment, new levels of behavior, new levels of responsibility and new levels of cognition - are again, a lot like new levels of technological capacity or scientific understanding: the foreign, uncharted lands they represent, the vast possibilities they bring to the forefront of one's conscious, are instinctively met with ambivalence and fear rather than curiosity or intrigue, no different than a primitive savage being introduced to fire for the first time.

Once more, the quest for productivity is an indirect path to a stronger identity. Thus, the final component to conquering yourself is embracing these psychological shifts, these subtle transitions in character and personal meaning that such a voyage entails. After the fact, you'll wonder how you ever tolerated what you'll come to view, retrospectively, as an inferior and uncivilized life.

Again, think of this book not simply as a manual for discipline and willpower, but as the beginning to a new literary ethos; as the genesis to an underlying framework for aspiring creative professionals who dare to remain self-directed in the digital age.

What you hold before you isn't simply a book, *it's a solution* of course: not just a single solution to an individual problem, but the beginning to an entirely new outlook on creative expression that's needed for the transitory sociological dynamics now underway.

The world is changing. We're fortunate enough to live in an exciting time of tremendous significance, which thus calls for tremendous adaptation. At the dawn of this new epoch, those who restructure their behavior <u>as well as their psyche</u> in ways to take advantage of its new roads - those who have not only talent and intelligence, <u>but also the discipline</u> to channel these traits in new ways - will perhaps rise into a new, "Knowledge Nobility": a creative aristocracy of social influence, power and wealth based neither on lineage nor political scheme, but simply on the depth of their creative intellect and the elegance of their internal-control.

---

[3] "It will make an immense difference in your faith and spirit, whether you look upon civilization as a good thing that is becoming better, or as a bad and evil thing that is decaying. One viewpoint gives you an advancing and expanding mind and the other gives you a descending and decreasing one...one viewpoint will make you grow greater and the other will inevitably cause you to grow small. One will enable you to work for the eternal things; the other will make you a mere patchwork reformer, working almost without hope to save a few lost souls from what you will grow to consider and lost and doomed world." ~ Wallace Wattles in his book <u>The Science of Being Great</u>.

But again, **knowledge and talent aren't enough.** Intelligence alone, or even immense intelligence and creativity in tandem, won't suffice. The conscious-creative thinker is in need of a third power, *discipline* - a unique form of composure and control which requires one to both see the world through a distinct frame of mind and construct one's goals with a distinct style of behavior. The strength to conquer one's creative potential, therefore, first begins with the strength to conquer one's self.

I hope you enjoyed this book, and that it's fulfilled your need for the wisdom, discipline and action-orientation which your creative goals demand of you in today's world. If you have any questions, or if any specific passages are unclear, simply email me, bryan@dotheknowledge.com, or visit my blog, dotheknowledge.com/transcend.

Peace…

"It is better to conquer yourself than to win a thousand battles. Then the victory is yours. It cannot be taken from you, not by demons or angels, heaven or hell…"
~ Buddha

COMPLETE LIST OF REFERENCES (BY ORDER OF MENTION)

The Tao Te Ching: Annotated and Explained by Lao Tzu and Derek Lin

Jonathan Livingston Seagull by Richard Bach

Bushido: The Soul of Japan by Inazo Nitobe

The Sword of No-Sword: Life of Master Warrior Tesshu by John Stephens

The Triune Brain in Evolution: Role in Paleocerebral Functions by Dr. Paul D. MacLean

The Dragons of Eden: Speculations on the Evolution of Human Intelligence by Carl Sagan

Life, the Movie: How Entertainment Conquered Reality by Neal Gabler

Consumed: How Markets Corrupt Children, Infantilize Adults and Swallow Citizens Whole by Benjamin R. Berber

The Hidden Persuaders by Vance Packard

Empire of Illusion: The End of Literacy and the Triumph of Spectacle by Christopher Hedges

The Now Habit: A Strategic Program for Ending Procrastination and Enjoying Guilt Free Play by Neil Fiore Ph.D

Mastery: Keys to Success and Long-Term Fulfillment by George Leonard

The Practicing Mind: Developing Discipline and Focus in Life by Thomas M. Sterner

Black Science: Ancient and Modern Ninja Techniques of Mind-Manipulation by Haha Lung and Christopher B. Prowant

Four Arguments for the Elimination of Television by Jerry Mander

The Science of Being Great by Wallace Wattles

The Fountainhead by Ayn Rand

Atlas Shrugged by Ayn Rand

Night of January 16th by Ayn Rand

Ideal by Ayn Rand

The Way of the Superior Man: A Spiritual Guide to Mastering the Challenges of Women, Work and Sexual Desire by David Deida

The Dragon Slayer with a Heavy Heart: A Powerful Story About Finding Happiness and Serenity…Even When You Really, Really Wish Some Things Were Different by Marcia Powers

Find Your Focus Zone: An Effective New Plan to Defeat Distraction and Overload by Lucy Jo Palladino

Wake Up Productive: Video Training Series by Eben Pagan

How to Get Focused by Scott Scheper and Nicola Franz

The Myth of Multitasking: How "Doing it All" Gets Nothing Done by Dave Crenshaw

Simpleology: The Simple Science of Getting Things Done by Mark Joyner

Hacking Your Education: Ditch the Lectures, Save Tens of Thousands and Learn More Then Your Peers Ever Will by Dale Stephens

Alone Together: How We Expect More From Technology and Less From Each Other by Sherry Turkle

The Visual Display of Quantitative Information by Edward R. Tufte

Quiet: The Power of Introverts in a World That Can't Stop Talking by Susan Cain

Willpower: Rediscovering the Greatest Human Strength by Dr. Roy Baumeister and John Tierney

The Willpower Instinct: How Self-Control Works, Why It Matters and What You Can Do to Get More of It by Kelly McGonigal

The Power of Full Engagement: Managing Energy, Not Time, is the Key to High Performance and Personal Renewal by Tony Schwartz and Jim Loehr

FOR MORE...

For more insight into the Conquer Yourself framework and methodology, set up a consultation session with me by emailing bryan@dotheknowledge.com or call direct at 718.577.1344.

Also, to install the principles of this book into the deep recesses of your mind, so that its contents become part of the automatic way you think, feel and behave (rather than eventually forget) order Think Right Now Intl.'s Accelerated Success Conditioning Software at dotheknowledge.com/think.

NOTES

NOTES

NOTES

NOTES

NOTES

Do The
Knowledge
DoTheKnowledge.com

Printed in Great Britain
by Amazon